THROUGH THE EYES OF LOVE

Other books by Lionel Whiston

Are You Fun to Live With?
Enjoy the Journey
New Beginnings: Relational Studies in Mark (1:1–4:34)
Power of a New Life: Relational Studies in Mark (4:35–9:50)
Through Suffering to Victory: Relational Studies in Mark (10:1–16:8)

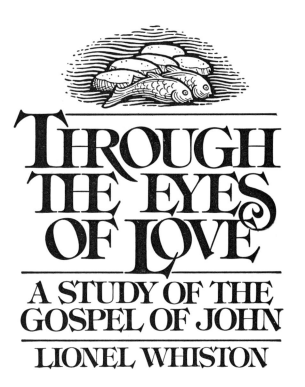

THROUGH THE EYES OF LOVE

A STUDY OF THE GOSPEL OF JOHN

LIONEL WHISTON

With grateful appreciation of our friends
in Wrentham, whose generosity in giving us
life residence in the "Whiston House"
made possible my wife, Irma's, and my conference
and retreat ministry in places near and far.

Contents

Introduction

I stand amazed before the Christ in the Gospel of John. He leaps out of the pages as the New Wine, the Living Water, the Living Bread, as Resurrection and Eternal Life. He moves from eternity to eternity. We see the Eternal God enfleshed and living in daily encounter with human beings— tender, angry, weak, strong, dying, forever alive.

When this Jesus of Nazareth is seen through the eyes of love, it is a soul-shaking experience that transforms, empowers and introduces an entirely new quality of life. As I have been studying this Gospel, Christ has become more strongly enthroned in my life, Shepherd of my soul, my food and my drink, the Guarantor of my future, my hope of resurrection and eternal life.

When I first started reading John's Gospel in preparation for this book, I struck impasse after impasse. For hours I sat without writing even a paragraph that was satisfactory.

I phoned my son in St. Louis, telling him of my dilemma. "I can't master this Gospel of John. I feel powerless before it," I said.

His answer was perceptive and provocative. "John's Gospel presents Jesus as the Christ and you can't master the Son of God. You can only let him master you." I had come seeking to understand and conquer, but instead Christ has conquered. He has shown me myself and I have felt understood, loved, forgiven and empowered. With reverent awe I can say, like Thomas, "My Lord and my God."

Each section of this book deals with a small portion of the Gospel, beginning with *Comment,* which seeks to discover the Gospel writer's intent and message, followed by *Reflection,* which places these truths in the contemporary situation of personal and corporate living. Scripture references, unless otherwise noted, are from the Revised Standard Version.

The structural pattern of the Gospel generally consists of an episode (which the Gospel writer designates as a *sign*) followed by a discourse. For instance, in chapter 4 the narrative, or sign, of Jesus at the well is followed by discourses on living water and true worship. In chapter 6 the narrative or sign is the feeding of the multitude followed by the discourse on the bread of life. The Passion (or Farewell) discourse (by far the longest in the Gospel) is somewhat different—narrative: 13:1–30; discourse: 13:31–17:26; narrative resumed: 18:1–19:42.

Key words occur throughout this Gospel, such as: *word* (mentioned only in the Prologue), *life* and *death, light* and *darkness, belief* and *unbelief, bread, water, glorify, truth, resurrection.* John makes frequent reference to "the Jews" as being opposed to Jesus. Many readers have thought the writer had an anti-Semitic bias. Not so! This Gospel was written about A.D. 100 when the early church and the synagogue were in conflict with each other. The issue is not that the Jews were Jews and to be withstood as such. Rather, John perceived them to be religious legalists, intent on keeping the letter of the Law and overlooking the deeper values of life. The parallel in our day would not be Jews, but persons or groups who are literalists, legalists about doctrine and procedures and opposed to the freedom of spirit and action that we see in Jesus.

The purpose of the Gospel is explicitly stated in 20:31. Out of a seemingly unlimited supply of material (21:25), the author has selected those incidents (signs) that show Jesus to be the Son of God so that people might believe in him, and believing have eternal life. The author of the Gospel wrote approximately three-quarters of a century after the events took place. As an old man, he dipped into the memories of the past recreating the scenes, seeing them with the eyes of love and interpreting them as the indwelling Christ revealed their meanings to him. I, in turn, have written this book on the Gospel of John so that Christ may again come alive for reader and writer alike, that together we may see the invisible Christ with the eyes of love and seeing, believe and have new life in him.

I have drawn freely on recent studies and commentaries on the Fourth Gospel. Anyone who knows this literature will recognize the influence of these authors on my thinking and wording in the pages which follow. In particular I have used with profit the following:

1. Charles H. Dodd, *The Interpretation of the Fourth Gospel* (Cambridge: University Press, 1953).
2. C. K. Barrett, *The Gospel According to St. John* (London: S.P.C.K., 1955).
3. Raymond E. Brown, *The Gospel According to John: The Anchor Bible,* vols. 29, 29A (New York: Doubleday, 1966, 1970).
4. Wilbert F. Howard, "Introduction and Exegesis to the

Introduction

Gospel According to St. John" in *The Interpreter's Bible,* ed. George A. Buttrick et al., vol. 8 (Nashville: Abingdon, 1952).

I am deeply grateful to my son, Dr. Lionel A. Whiston, Jr., of Eden Theological Seminary, St. Louis, for his great help and critical insights. Much credit is due him. My wife, Irma, has given skillful literary advice. My secretary, Phyllis Bailey, has labored over my handwriting and patiently typed and retyped! My thanks to them and to countless friends who have given me encouragement. I have especially appreciated the critical and editorial helpfulness of Robin Hardy of Word Books as well as the warm cooperation of that company in publishing and promoting my books.

Lionel (Lee) Whiston

Wrentham, Massachusetts
1980

I

The Prologue
(John 1:1–18)

In the Beginning . . .

Read John 1:1–18

Comment: What affirmation, what rhapsody is in this Prologue! Like an overture it suggests the great themes that are dealt with in this Gospel. It is written from the viewpoint of one seeing the ascended Christ in the midst of the early church.

Verses 1–2. At once we sense the cosmic sweep of "in the beginning," as in Genesis 1:1. At the outset John affirms the eternal coexistence of the Word (i.e., the Christ) with God. "Word" (Greek, *Logos*) meant *divine principle,* or *wisdom* to the Greeks. The Jews, however, were reminded of the *Word of the Lord:* "He spoke and it was done." Jesus was this Word from God. God and Jesus are "with" each other. They are one.

Verse 3. Everything in existence bears the stamp of the Spirit of Christ. The universe is made for cooperation and coherence, not hate and disintegration; it is a universe not a multiverse.

Verse 4. Life! Jesus was truly alive and his life was a

beacon light to humankind. The life of Jesus was the light by which men were to walk into a new dimension of being. The life of Jesus, like light, revealed the dark places as blacker and the visible places as brighter. Jesus showed people their selves as they were, but also the selves that they might become.

Verses 6–8. An interlude referring to John the Baptist. We leave cosmic history for an incident in human history.

Verse 9. *True* light. He is not merely light, but the *true* light, the embodiment of truth (see 14:6).

Verses 10–13. These are among the saddest words of the Bible. The world he loved and the men he came to enlighten turned against him! (see Isa. 53:3, 4). But to those who received him and believed him to be the Christ, the Son of God, he gave *power to become* children of God. A new seed of life, a new center of being mysteriously comes to dwell within. We no longer lay claim to illustrious forebears. It is no longer merely a biological birth with programmed genes and tendencies. It is not the extended purposes and ego strength of earthly parents or the drive of human will power, our own or others'. Our parentage is from above. God through Christ is saying, "I am willing to risk myself with you." Divine love has adopted us, put his Spirit in our lives, his strength in our bodies. We are children of God born of him, made new, destined to be becomers and overcomers.

Verse 14. Here is the key verse of the Prologue. This eternal Christ, the Son of God, empties himself of all prerogatives and takes on human form and relates to us as a fellow human being. Yet shining through this flesh in word and deed is the glory of God. Only one born of God could be so glorious, so full of grace and truth. Grace is the feminine counterpart, truth the masculine counterpart of the human personality. Both find their full and balanced expression in Jesus.

Verse 15 returns to John the Baptist and the Baptism of Jesus.

Verse 16. The word *fulness* suggests that the nature of Jesus' ministry was not one of strain and stress, but an overflow of the Person that he really was. Grace is love expressed or love in action. Through the presence of Jesus Christ we receive unmerited love upon love—unending waves of the gracious acts of God.

Verse 17. Moses' legacy was the Law with its complex web of commandments and rules—the Law that left people with guilt and frustration, or, on the other hand, with a smug complacency of keeping minuscule rules while neglecting the deeper relationships of life. God's legacy through Jesus Christ was grace and truth. A gracious love that redeems and affirms, a truth that keeps us in touch with the realities of life.

Verse 18. Again the oneness and intimacy of God and his Son are emphasized—a relationship that holds the key to understanding much in this Gospel. It is because of this close relationship that Jesus can make known his Father and interpret him.

The remainder of the Gospel is an extension of what is contained in the Prologue.

Reflection: The wisdom of the ages now lives in history. But only those who believe will recognize him. We are invited not merely to see a man Jesus, but One who is the Logos of God. Jesus Christ is the embodiment of the Divine principle running through this universe. What does this say to you about the nature of ultimate reality? Is it fate, "red tooth and claw," chance, or caring love?

Since Christ and God are one, how does this affect your

view of the nature of God? Of the nature of Jesus Christ?

At nighttime things often look darker and problems blacker to me. In the morning life is brighter. Christ is both my life and my light. As my fellowship with him deepens and strengthens, the way looks brighter and I walk with assurance.

Verse 11. Ever have your friends go back on you? Particularly those for whom you have cared deeply? Jesus experienced this too. Such a thought gives me great comfort.

Verses 12–13. We are all "becomers" in him. *Growth* in Christ, not attainment, is the evidence of life. To what source do you trace your personality traits, your temperament, your views of life? What bloodstream flows through your soul?

Verse 14. When people behold us what do they see? Grace is love, and truth is honesty. Jesus was *full* of love and truth. My wife and I embody these virtues in varying degrees. I tend to be long on love and short on honesty. She is as honest as the day is long, but could be more loving at times!

II

The Self-Revelation of Jesus
(John 1:19–4:54)

John the Baptist Bears Witness

Read John 1:19–34

Comment: In the Prologue the author of this Gospel bore witness that Jesus was the Eternal Word made flesh, Life that was the true Light of men, the only Son from the Father. In the remainder of chapter one (vv. 19–51) he recounts how John the Baptist and some of Jesus' disciples bore witness to who this Jesus was. Later the author selects signs and discourses further to support this witness.

Verses 19–23. John the Baptist was honest as to who he himself was. He wanted none of the honor that rightly belonged to Jesus. In a wilderness world of confusion and lostness, he announces the coming of the Lord of life.

Verses 24–28. John was a forerunner, an announcer. He emphasized that he was unworthy to do the lowliest of services, even to untie the thong of the sandal of the One to come. Rabbi Joshua ben Levi, writing in the third century, said, "Every service which a slave performs for his master a pupil will do for his teacher, except loosing his shoe." (Quoted by Howard, "Introduction and Exegesis to the Gospel according to St. John," 8:482. For full information on this and following references, see the Introduction.)

Verses 29–34. John the Baptist announced that Jesus was to be the world's sin bearer, the Lamb of God, that Jesus would baptize with the Holy Spirit, and finally that Jesus was the Son of God, i.e., the Messiah, the One sent from God.

Reflection: John gives us a lesson in genuine humility. He describes his work and mission candidly with a view to honoring Jesus and not himself. He is not worthy to perform the most menial of tasks, untying Jesus' shoes! A requisite for genuine humility is an honest appraisal of one's own worth and also a willingness to live so that credit is reflected on another and not oneself.

Reflect on your appreciation of your own worth; whether the aim of your life is to bring glory to yourself or directed toward building up others; whether you want center stage and to receive the praise for yourself or to be an affirmer of others, making possible their joy and honor. When I do a kindness I often find lurking within me a desire that people will know about it even if I have to tell them myself! Ever feel that way?

Verses 32–34. Recall when you have been exposed to some expression of the greatness of God: inspiring music, towering mountain peaks, the recital of a great creed, a great passage of Scripture, a soul-stirring drama. Has something in you responded deeply? Have you affirmed God's majesty? His forgiving grace? His caring love? Reread the Prologue (vv. 1–18), this majestic tribute to the glory of the Christ. What affirmations rise up within you? At what points are you crying out, "It is true, yes, I know it is true"? John the Baptist bore his witness to the Christ; what is yours?

Come and See

Read John 1:35-51

Comment: Five disciples are mentioned: Andrew, Simon Peter, an unnamed disciple (possibly John), Philip and Nathanael.

Verses 35-37. John the Baptist further exemplified his unselfishness as he pointed out "the Lamb of God," knowing full well that his disciples might leave him to follow Jesus, as indeed they did.

Verses 38, 39. "What do you seek?" or "What realities of living are you searching for?" The reply, "Where are you staying?" was tantamount to saying, "We want to know more about you."

Verses 40-42. Andrew is mentioned twice more in this Gospel: 6:8 and 12:22. Jesus renamed Simon. He was to be *Cephas* (the Aramaic for *rock*), prophetic of the change that was to take place in his character.

Verses 43-50. Nathanael lived only a few miles from Nazareth, and together with his neighbors, was evidently condescending toward the inhabitants of this village. In verse 46 Philip used the words Jesus himself had spoken in verse 39, "Come and see." "Under [a] fig tree" (v. 48) was sometimes referred to by rabbis as the best place to study God's word. Nathanael's study of the Scriptures was small in comparison to what he would see, as for example, the miracle at Cana (probably Nathanael's hometown).

Verse 51. A symbolic way of saying that the Christ came from God and would return to him, and also that the communication between God and his Son would be continuous and dynamic. "Son of man" is Jesus' way of referring to himself in this Gospel.

Reflection: Verse 36. What deep personal experiences enable you to say, "Behold, the Lamb of God who takes away the sins of the world"? What sins of yours has he taken or is taking away? What happens as you verbalize your faith in Jesus?

Verse 38. Three of us had had breakfast together for five years. One of our number was offered a position in the West. At our last meal together he said to the two of us, "What do you want me to pray for when I remember you in prayer?" He wanted his prayers to reach our inner depths. Jesus asked searchingly, "What do you really seek? What is your deepest need?"

Verse 39. Jesus did not say, "Listen and I will tell you" but "Come and see." Do people see the Spirit of Christ in us and our work?

Verse 42. Note Jesus' affirmation and upgrading of Simon. Jesus saw the potential of stability in one who must have been known in his community as an emotional hothead. What is your custom—downgrading, boxing in, noting another's faults; or upgrading, enhancing and affirming latent potentials in people? In what ways can you grow in discovering and affirming the skills of others?

Note the witness borne by the disciples: John the Baptist repeats "Behold, the Lamb of God" (v. 36). Andrew affirms Jesus to be the Messiah (v. 41). It takes courage to witness to your own family! Philip told Nathanael that they had found the One of whom Moses and the prophets wrote, i.e., the Messiah (v. 45). Nathanael declares, "Rabbi, you are the Son of God" (v. 49). What is your endorsement of this Christ?

In the following sections (2:1–4:42) we see that apparently casual incidents—a wedding feast, a Passover celebration, a counseling session, a woman drawing water—became crucial for people when Jesus encountered them. He brought new wine, promised a new temple, showed the way for new birth, and offered living water. The new wine, the new birth, the living water symbolized the newness of life present at that very moment in him, for he embodied them in his own Person. Those who believed in him embraced this newness of being; their lives were changed. Those who did not believe remained bound in their old imprisoning traditions.

The New Wine of the Spirit
Read John 2:1–11

Comment: Jesus was the kind of a person one would want to have around at a wedding. He came to bring life and joy to the party.

The reason the writer included this story in the Gospel was that people might know that Jesus was the Son of God and might believe in him (see Introduction and 20:31). This actually happened at Cana (v. 11), where Jesus "manifested his glory." "We have beheld his glory" (see 1:14).

Verse 11. A *sign* in this Gospel is a deed or narrative that points beyond itself. A sign on a highway, for instance, points to the immediate situation: a crossroad or a railroad. Signs here are symbols, having hidden meanings. This account of Jesus' turning water into wine is not to impress us with a miraculous deed, but to point out that newness of life (the wine of the Spirit) is available for us in Christ.

The greatest of the signs, the death on the cross, was not just the killing of a good man, but God's love and salvation made available to all men through Christ. The incident at Cana is the first of the signs with hidden meanings around which John structures his Gospel.

Reflection: Is your religion making you attractive so that people like to have you around? A dedicated Christian woman was constantly invited to parties in Washington, D.C., and always drank tomato juice for her cocktail. Her friends often said, "Elaine, you get more kick out of your drink than we do out of a dozen of our kind. You're the life of the party." How can you be more fun and joy around the home, the job—anywhere?

To all of us Christ, as the Son of God, offers the wine of the Spirit. Think of ways in which you may drink more deeply of Christ: in the morning as you awaken, as you drive to work, as you take the cup at the Communion Service. The living Christ is present as much in the most casual as in the most significant event of your day.

Make a list of some things in your lifestyle that could be included under "old wine," such as holding on to worn-out customs, unwillingness to be real, resistance to change. Now make a second list suggested by "new wine" such as a new freedom, an inner joy.

The old Jewish way of keeping the countless traditions and laws of the past finds its counterpart in us today when we are controlled by the red lights of inhibitions, past customs, and a static mental attitude. The new life in Christ finds us responding more and more to the green lights of freedom, expression, exploration and creativity.

Facing Institutional Corruption

Read John 2:12–25

Comment: The story of the cleansing of the Temple stands in marked juxtaposition to the Cana wedding story. These stories reflect Old Testament thinking of rewards and judgments. The wedding bids us welcome and is an occasion of joy. The Temple cleansing expresses God's anger at disobedience. The Gospel of John frequently uses contrasting values: light and darkness, belief and unbelief, acceptance and rejection, life and death.

This sign of the Temple cleansing moves on two levels of meaning, as does the Cana story. At the wedding feast, we have seen that the old wine and the new symbolized the difference between the meticulous keeping of the religious laws in contrast to the new life and freedom of the Spirit in Christ. Here the obvious meaning is that Jesus somehow would demolish this great structure, the Temple, and rebuild it in three days. The hidden and true implication was that the Jewish mode of worship which placed legalism and ritual above human values would be replaced by a better form, a life-giving fellowship rooted in Christ. This would be the new "Temple." This hidden truth would become manifest when he was raised from the dead (v. 22).

Reflection: Jesus' criticisms of Judaism came from one who was a loyal Jew and stood within the framework of that which he attacked. When we are dissatisfied with the church or any other institution (home, school or business) of which we are a part, do we desert it, become disloyal and attack it from without? Or do we stay with our group, laboring more earnestly and lovingly when things go against us? We forfeit the right to be heard when we speak from outside a situation.

Recall some situation where everything seemed to have gone wrong in the church (or some other institution). Did you pull out or stay with it? Did your words come from one who "stood within," caring for and loyal to the church or institution? Talk about ways of bringing about change, when and where it is right to be angry, yet how to continue in love, loyal to the end—even as was Jesus.

This story has to do with those who accent church loyalty and worship and yet neglect moral values and the welfare of persons. The Holocaust that killed six million Jews was perpetrated for the most part by so-called Christians, often fathers of families! We know now the ghastly events of the Vietnamese war. What was your attitude toward the war? In the light of subsequent revelations, would you keep that same attitude?

In Jesus' day, under the cloak of celebrating the Passover, people were exploiting others for personal gain. In today's world what is the living Christ saying to us who live in an affluent society amid a world of hunger? What is the church's responsibility toward human rights, e.g., the torturing of political prisoners in many countries? The denial of justice in many cases to minority groups in the United States?

Born from Above

Read John 3:1–21

Comment: This section begins with Nicodemus coming under the darkness of night (v. 2) and ends with the announcement of the Light that takes away the darkness of the world (vv. 19–21).

Verses 3–4. The Greek word for "born anew" also carries the meaning "born again" and "born from above." Nicodemus can only comprehend biological birth. Jesus, however, is not speaking of a repetition of earthly birth, but being born of dual parentage, an earthly and a heavenly Father (see 1:13).

Verse 6. For John the word *flesh* means of earthly or human origin, not "evil" as with St. Paul and many contemporary Christians.

Verses 8–9. In Hebrew, Greek and Old English alike one word was used for "wind," "breath" and "spirit": *ruach, pneuma,* and *gast,* respectively (cf. Holy Gast or Holy Ghost). Just as the wind with its unpredictable nature cannot be charted, so the Breath of the Spirit with its spontaneity and surprise blows in our lives. Small wonder that Nicodemus, bound by rules and duties, could not comprehend this windlike freedom of the Spirit!

Verses 14–15. The snake-bitten Israelites, confused and lost in the wilderness, threatened with death, looked to the serpent God had ordered Moses to raise (Num. 21:9 ff.). In like manner confused persons bitten by despair and darkness will look at the Son of man who was to be raised up on the Cross by the same God. To look on the brazen serpent brought earthly life. To look on Jesus and believe was to receive eternal life.

Verse 16. This verse is one of the gems of the Bible. It tells of the great gift of a loving God. This gift, as all biblical gifts, is conditional however on our faith—and faith includes obedience.

God's great love for all of his children is shown by his sending his only Son not only to come to us in the flesh (Incarnation), but also to die for us and to rise from the dead (the Atonement and Resurrection). Faith in this Son gives a new quality of life, life from above. It is a life not dependent on circumstances, or the limitations of space and time. It is a life of freedom, of joy. It is not a life of restraint, legalism and keeping rules, but one of adventure, response and obedience to the love of God. John calls this *eternal life.* We note that something had happened to Nicodemus when later in the Gospel he courageously stood by Jesus (see 7:50; 19:39).

Verse 17. God's purpose in sending his Son was to *save* the world, opening the way to eternal life through his Son (see Ezek. 18:31, 32).

Verse 18. In rejecting this offer of life, persons by their own decision-making sentence themselves. God wills to save us, but by our refusal to believe we condemn ourselves.

25

Verses 19–21. They loved (i.e., preferred) darkness rather than light. Jesus came as the "light" of the world and as "truth." To reject Jesus was to reject both light and truth, and therefore to live in darkness and to be condemned. To "do the truth" (v. 21) and to "do falsehood" (v. 20) are Jewish idioms. Truth and falsehood are conceived not as intellectual positions, but as lifestyles. To "do the truth" leads to insight, understanding and light; to "do falsehood" leads to unreality and darkness.

Thus the story of Nicodemus begins in the darkness of night and ends in the glowing light of the Christ.

Reflection: There is so much in this chapter, it is like trying to put the ocean in a child's sand pail. Let your imagination play with the words "Born from above . . . anew . . . again . . . from above." How does it happen? Is there a passivity? A shock of recognition? It is not something you do, but something that is done to you.

There is our part, of course: repentance, willingness to change, cutting the umbilical cord of the past, going on to the adventure of faith. Then there is God's part: offering forgiveness to blot out our guilt; adding the unlimited resources of the Spirit to the limitations of the flesh; giving certainty for confusion, light for darkness, life for death, freedom of the Spirit for bondage to tradition. Dream of what it means to have this invasion from above, this rebirth of the Spirit.

Verse 8. My grandson was skating recently. He said, "I watched the passing scene: youngsters learning, lovers hand in hand, others gliding by with confidence, some with puck and hockey sticks. The surroundings changed as trees and landmarks passed by. Suddenly I threw up my head and saw the stars, fixed points amid the changing scene. I thought of God as the fixed point in my life and in a moment felt the surety and serenity of eternity pass into my life." The Spirit comes so unexpectedly. We cannot predict it— an infant's smile, a quiet thought, a revolutionary idea— and lo, the Spirit has come! What things and incidents have occasioned a birth of the Spirit in you?

Verses 14–16. The heart of the Gospel is here: God who loves and gives of himself in Jesus even to the death! When we encounter this limitless love what is our response? The Israelites looked to the brazen serpent and lived. We, look- ing at and believing in the crucified Jesus, may have not merely physical but eternal life here and now. What part did or does the fear of perishing play (v. 16)? The joy of reward (eternal life)? The haunting pull of the love of Christ on the cross? The desire to love and serve others?

Verses 17, 18. I am one of those who for years thought God sent Jesus to judge and condemn me. His perfect life gave me a feeling of guilt. I have done an about-face in my thinking. I began to sense God's love instead of judgment of me when I personalized verses 16 and 17 in this manner, "God so loved Lee Whiston that he gave his only Son, that, as Lee Whiston believes in him, Lee Whiston does not perish but has eternal life. For God did not send his Son to condemn Lee Whiston, but that Lee Whiston through him might be saved." What happens when you put *your* name in these verses? or the names of others?

Verses 19–21. I find in myself a constant desire to "play games," to live behind a mask, to hide part of myself deep within. To this extent I prefer to live in darkness rather than the light. I shun the light lest I should expose the real me that is inside.

When I am willing to live in openness with my fellow beings (i.e., "walk in the light"), then I have nothing to hide for I live as one who is newborn and free.

What is your experience with living behind a mask? Taking continual flights into fantasy and unreality? What is your experience as you have sought to live in openness?

The Choice Is Always Ours

Read John 3:22–36

Comment: This section suggests options: In our relationships we have the choice of self-advancement versus the kind of humility and loyalty we see in John the Baptist. We can seek our strength from earthly sources or from the One who comes to us from above. We can choose between darkness and light, death and newness of birth.

The scene shifts to the Jordan River. John the Baptist speaks concerning his relationship to Jesus.

Verse 29. References to the bridegroom may well allude to the Cana story (2:1–11).

Reflection: The heart of the Baptist's message is in the words, "He must increase, but I must decrease." It is as if he were saying, "Whatever there is of real value in either of us has been given to us by God. Don't worry. Let's be thankful for what is." Contrast this attitude with the desire for one-upmanship and the power plays that creep into our life situations. How can we so live in our daily relationships that we decrease and the spirit of Christ increases? In our parenting, does our authority as adults decrease so that the children may mature? Likewise, does a teacher or a leader in business or church circles "decrease" by delegating tasks and advancing others so that they may gain experience and identity? Does jealousy ever keep you from this largeness of spirit? When I have been plagued with jealousy I have found that thanking God for the other person—often my wife—brings victory!

Note in contrast the need at times to claim authority as Jesus did when cleansing the Temple (2:13–16). Give examples of when you were right in assuming authority in one situation and in relinquishing it in another. What does this say to you?

Verses 31–36. Because of our humanity we are from "below," "of the earth." The miracle of faith in Christ is this: that the One who comes from above, even Jesus Christ, abides in us. Speak of your experience when this Spirit from above has broken through in some casual or maybe some significant events in your life. To desire Christ to dwell in your life and to believe he guides and empowers is the heart of John's Gospel. I start out in the morning believing this and, wow! What a difference! Yes, I slip and have to begin again and again, but this is what it's all about. I am human but also I bear the divine stamp.

In verse 36 we are given the option of belief or unbelief, obedience or disobedience. To believe and to incorporate this belief into our manner of living is to move by faith from the darkness in which we are trapped into the light and presence of God's Spirit. To disbelieve and disobey is to continue in self-defeating legalism bound by man-made rules and regulations. Thus chapter 3 moves between two sets of poles: the poles of darkness in which Nicodemus approaches Jesus (v. 2) and the Light of the world (v. 19); and the poles of birth into life (v. 3) and disobedience into death (v. 36). The choice is always ours.

Chapter 4 moves from thirst to living water, hunger to harvest, the hostility of a lone woman to the acclaim of her compatriots, the localized worship of Mount Gerizim and Jerusalem to the universal sweep of Spirit and Truth as embodied in Christ.

Jesus, Counselor *Par Excellence*
Read John 4:1–26

Comment: Verses 7–10. What a natural opening, beginning at the level of the woman's interests! It is difficult for us to sense the depths of hatred between Jews and Samaritans (the Mideast was, and is, a place of much bitterness). Yet Jesus envisioned the woman as one worthy and capable of receiving the message of new life, and later he declares his Messianic nature to her.

Water—the flowing, cool water of Jacob's well, or Jesus' gift of living water! Here we see again John's artful use of a word with two levels of meaning. With what adroitness ("If you knew") Jesus intrigued her, leading her step by step until in verse 15 she was saying to him, this hated Jew, "Give me this water."

Verses 11–15. She parried with him and then unsheathed her best weapon. It was *Jacob's* well. "Are you greater than our father Jacob?" The irony of it was, she did not know that Jesus was indeed greater! Jesus met her head-on. "This water quenches thirst but only for a time. The water which I can give you satisfies forever." The woman does not comprehend; her reply is still on the earthly level: " . . . that I may not . . . come here to draw." Nevertheless she is intrigued and open.

Verses 16–20. To be able to receive the living water, she must first face her sin. Jesus looked deep in her heart (see 2:25) and found a vulnerable spot. She was honest, confessed the truth and then avoided dealing with her sin as she trailed off into a theological argument. John, as he often does, has used the narrative to initiate a theological discourse: Where to worship? Mount Gerizim, the mountain sacred to the Samaritans, or Mount Zion (Jerusalem), sacred to the Jews?

Reflection: Verse 6. It was very important to John that his readers feel the humanity of Jesus—tired, thirsty, exhausted with the heat of the day, also angry in 2:15–17. Can you see much of your own humanity in him?

Verses 7–10. Note Jesus' style of approach to this woman. He said enough to intrigue without pressuring. What is your approach? Intriguing? Nonpressuring? Thoughtless? Insensitive? Antagonizing? Do you accentuate differences or discover common ground?

Verses 11–16. Jesus refused to get involved in a theological debate about the greatness of "our father Jacob" but bore witness to the living water. What does this say of your style of witness and conversation? Do you argue about religion? Or do you witness of what God is doing in your life? Do you sense the right moment and have the courage to ask a penetrating question? Note there is no condemnation in Jesus' words.

Verse 19. Do you have a willingness to speak the truth bravely or a tendency to continue to play games and avoid being honest? Think also of how Jesus carefully prepared the situation so that not only could he speak, but she was ready (at least in some measure) to respond.

The searching heart of the woman symbolized by her multiple husbands finds its answer in Christ. I have discovered that sin in my life is often a perverted hunger for God. When she was made whole she saw people not as a means to her wholeness, but as ready to receive her witness, "ripe for harvest."

Where are you searching for wholeness? In work? In success? Making people—children, pupils, peers—to serve your ends? How does wholeness in Christ change your relationships with persons?

Here were people (the Jews and Samaritans) who lived in close proximity, yet could not worship together. Where is this happening today? Why don't people in the same congregation like each other? Why can't all Christians take the Sacrament together? How do we begin to rebuild these relationships?

What are the factors that tend to divide Christians today? In what ways are we bound to our parochial theologies or practices, whether liberal or conservative, that separate us from other children of God? Do we tend to feel superior about the way we worship? What does it mean to worship together "in spirit and in truth"?

Is This Not the Christ?

Read John 4:27–42

Comment: Verse 27. The disciples on their return failed to be forthright with Jesus. They hid their feelings, stifled their questions, "played games."

Verse 29. "Come, see"—this phrase is used here for the third time (see 1:39, 46). "Come, see" is so much more effective than "come, hear." People are more apt to respond to one who models his message. The one who can reveal our inner selves to us immediately commands our attention and respect. Jesus did just this.

Verses 34–36. Implicit in the simple sentence of verse 34 is the sense of mission that Jesus had in his work and his complete obedience to his Father. When we have helped others into the Christian life or been the instruments of their growth we share a common joy (i.e., "rejoice together").

Few joys equal that of two people discovering Christ or growing in him together (see 1 John 1:3, 4).

Verse 39. After this discourse about food and harvest we again have the reference to believing in Christ. This is John's purpose in writing the Gospel (20:31). The woman was a changed individual—honest, confessing her faults, excited about the One who helped her to discover herself.

Verses 41–42. The message was no longer secondhand. The Samaritans now have had firsthand, direct contact with Jesus.

Reflection: Verses 33–34. As Jesus contrasted old and new wine, earthly water and living water, so now he speaks of physical food for earthly life versus spiritual food for eternal life. The disciples find it difficult to think in terms of the spirit, even as did Nicodemus (3:9, 12). To have ministered to this woman's need was as food to his soul; it was doing God's will and accomplishing his work. For most of us our hunger for two or three square meals a day takes precedence over everything else. Jesus spoke of satisfying another hunger: ministering to God's needy children. To him it was exciting and immediate. What are the hungers in your life? The fields are white for harvest. Lonely, frustrated lives are everywhere. We assume that a smiling face covers a joyous heart, a prosperous bank account indicates a fulfilled man, a new house implies a happy home. It is not always so!

Children eager for a listening ear come home from school. Do we immediately seek to fit them into our plans ("Now get your music practice done"), or do we listen awhile?

Someone seeks me out at the close of an exhausting conference session, or sits next to me on a crowded plane as I travel homeward. I don't want to talk to them; or worse,

I listen with a divided mind, thinking, *How long will this last? I want to relax now.* And opportunities to minister are lost! What fields ready for harvest are we overlooking?

People of Authority

Read John 4:43–54

Comment: This official was accustomed to having his own way and being adequate. He finds himself in a situation he cannot handle, and comes to Jesus. Jesus exercises the same kind of authority over death and illness as the official used in his political life. The climax of this story is reached when the man and his household declare their belief in Christ (see 20:31).

In this story, as in the Lazarus and Passion narratives, the Gospel writer is showing Jesus as the Lord of life and Victor over death.

Reflection: What are the authority figures in your life? Teacher? Parent? Boss? Family patterns? Childhood training? What is the role of Christ in relation to these other authorities? Does he affirm them? Would he change or supersede them?

Jesus, who showed his authority in cleansing the Temple and healing this boy, was also himself obedient to the will of his Father. Consider the quality of authority in your life as enriched by your willingness to be obedient. In which places is Christ the authority in your life? In which is he not?

Sickness of mind or body often breeds fear. A persistent and perhaps desperate turning to Christ (v. 49) brings peace and often healing. The miracles may not always happen as we wish. But persistent, overcoming faith in Christ is often the prelude to his amazing deeds. What is your experience?

I was taken sick in Bethlehem, Pennsylvania, and rushed to the hospital, delirious with 106-degree temperature. A friend phoned my wife in New England, "Lee is unconscious, Irma. But I am an R.N. I will 'special' him and phone you as soon as he is conscious. He will need you then." My wife went to her rocking chair and told the Lord all about it! She found she could not pray for me to get well, but could only keep thanking God for our fifty-two years of married life and love. A deep peace came over her. She waited patiently. In forty-eight hours the call came for her to come to Bethlehem. Jesus Christ is Lord of life.

III

Signs and Controversies
(John 5:1–9:41)

The Word of Life

Read John 5:1–18

Comment: We have two successive stories of healing: that of the official's son (4:46–54) and now this one of the man beside the Pool of Bethzatha.

Picture the scene: The man had lain there thirty-eight years, longer than the total expected life span of those days. He lay hovering between the fear of death and the hope of life. Each year another had reached the healing waters before him. Note that Jesus did not do the healing for the man until he responded to Jesus with an obedient act of faith.

Jesus recognized that the claim of human need took primacy over the legalistic restrictions regarding the Sabbath. This offended the religious authorities and brought down their wrath upon him. He further angered them by calling God his Father. For the Jews this was blasphemy, but for John, Jesus' equality with God was of prime importance.

Reflection: How often the phrase crossed the man's lips, "There is no one . . . there is no one." Most of us feel like this at one time or another. Elijah moaned, "I only, am left"

(1 Kings 19:10). Paul came near to that point, "Demas has deserted me . . . only Luke is with me" (2 Tim. 4:10, 11). This is when self-pity sets in. We scurry around to find sympathy or security. We lose hope and are immobilized, unaware that at this very moment Christ is here, nearer than breathing, offering us life.

Like the man beside the Pool, we too can be only partially alive—part of us dead in spirit or body and part of us alive. In what places are we beginning to die? In the lessening of joy? The writing off of hopes? The foregoing of dreams? The giving in to the inertias of body and soul? Christ is calling us to lay aside all deadness of spirit and constant apprehension of sickness of body and come alive in him who is the Lord of life. What is Jesus asking you to do in order to be whole? What can the words *rise, carry,* and *walk* mean to you?

I find it is easy to use pain or feelings of rejection as an excuse for withdrawal. In times of illness I often think, "Do I really want to get well and be engaged in the battle of life?" To say yes to the power of Christ is to find the faith to stand up and walk tall in God's strength.

Note the *tough* love of Jesus. He does not take the man's hand and help him to rise. He does not even offer to carry his pallet for him! He knows that there is unused power resident within the man. Christ commands us today to come alive in him, to tackle the impossible. Do we have the faith to do this? In our relations with others is our love too sentimental? Does our helping people weaken or strengthen them?

The Father Gives Life Through the Son
Read John 5:19–29

Comment: Verses 19–21. Note the humility of Jesus and his dependence on God. These words of Jesus refer back to the healings of the boy (4:46–54) and of the man by the Pool Bethzatha (5:1–18). Their common theme is that God is continually giving life to mankind. He has given his Son the power to lift us out of death into life (see especially v. 21).

Verses 22–25. It is by faith in the Son that people are no longer under judgment nor even under the threat of death, but have passed out of death into life. This is not a future event only, but takes place in the present situation and the now moment. The word *life* (see 10:10) denotes a fullness of living that Christ the Son gives us now and will give us forever. Death has no power to conquer or interrupt this kind of life.

Verses 28–29 refer not only to the Final Judgment, but to a quickening of all who are spiritually dead in the Church. This narrative is not just about a Jesus who healed an invalid in Judea, but of a Christ who can and will raise all who believe in him to newness of life and power.

Reflection: This section describes God as forever working on our behalf, bringing us out of death into life. He has given this life-giving power to his Son, Jesus Christ, who in turn brings life to us as we believe in him and obey him.

I find at least three areas in my life where I am apt to be under judgment and I need a continuing power to move from death to life. My childhood tapes run overtime. I recall hearing: "Now be careful, I know you'll drop it." "If there's a wrong way to do a thing you'll find it." Therefore I tend to set unrealistically high goals for myself and then feel guilty when I fail to reach them. To be set free from this bondage of the past is to move from death to life. Christ is doing this for me.

Again, when God has blessed me or my work, I tend to

interpret it in terms of personal success and start to play God, thinking I am adequate to run my life. For example, after success as a counselor I sometimes assume I have all the answers. So often the next person who comes to me pays the price for my conceit as I am unable to help. Once more I need the Christ to free me from myself.

Finally, sin seeks to find a lodging place in me in terms of power plays and self-centered moods, desires and fantasies. I find myself on the one hand seeking to gain one-upmanship in encounters, and on the other hand withdrawing into negative attitudes. Then I know my only hope is in turning to Christ who leads me from death to life. What is your experience?

Jesus Cites the Evidence

Read John 5:30–47

Comment: Jesus claimed that his judgment was "just" on four counts: (1) He sought to do God's will and not his own (v. 30); (2) John the Baptist testified that Jesus was the Christ (vv. 31–33); (3) The works Jesus did, bringing wholeness to the sick boy (4:46–54) and to the invalid man (5:1–18), testified that he was sent from God (that is, sent "from above" not "from below," see 3:3); (4) Moses bore witness to Jesus (vv. 45–47).

Jesus asserts that the religious leaders will not believe in him and therefore cannot recognize God's voice or presence in him. If they had read the Scriptures aright, not with literalism and legalism, but in the Spirit of God they would have seen that the Old Testament points to Jesus as the Christ. But they would not do this. He adds, "If I came glorifying myself you would believe me. But my glory is from God."

Reflection: In this passage Jesus claims to be the Christ, the Messiah, the Son of God. How do we respond to this?

Verse 30. Christ chose to be controlled by God. Who is in charge of your life? What is the evidence for this?

Verse 32. John the Baptist bore witness of Jesus. Are there those who can bear witness of your Christian life? How about your family? Fellow motorists? Fellow club members? Business associates? What would they say? "If you were arrested for being a Christian, would there be enough evidence to convict you?"

Verse 36. This Christ does works of healing. What healing is taking place in you? Between you and others?

Verse 40. Christ is the giver of life, abundant life. Is this life entering into your being? What is happening?

Verses 45–47. The religious leaders read their Bible, literally, seeking out passages to support their traditions and ancient customs. How do you read yours? To support what you already know and to entrench you more deeply in your position, or to recognize in it the story of Christ, the Giver of life? Life means growth. Peter, writing to Christians in the early church, said, "Grow up into salvation" (1 Pet. 2:2). What evidences are there in your life of growth and of the flow of the Spirit of life as we know it in Christ?

The Bread of Life

Read John 6:1–15

Comment: Verse 5. Jesus saw people not as interrupters, but as offering an opportunity for caring and service.

Verses 8–9. Andrew, entrepreneur extraordinaire! He is mentioned three times in this Gospel: 1:40–42; 6:8 and 12:22. On each of these three occasions he is bringing someone to Jesus!

How often Jesus ate with people. He was "known in the breaking of bread." This sign, the feeding of the multitude, remains just another miracle until we see it on two levels. It reveals Jesus to us as "the prophet who is to come into the world!" (v. 14), and the Bread of life (v. 35).

Reflection: Do people in general annoy you? If I am busy with my plans or program and people want to see me, I am often tempted to regard them as interrupters and resent their intrusion. But if I can see these people in terms of their needs and hungers rather than as interrupters then my heart goes out to them and I find it easy to minister to them. Mark tells us (6:34) that Jesus saw them as "sheep without a shepherd." He saw them in terms of needs, not in terms of their faults.

Verse 14. After they had eaten, some of the people saw in the incident a "sign"; a deeper meaning was present beneath the partaking of a meal. Are there similar overtones and insights as you eat at the family table? Is there a picture of Jesus on your dining room wall, or a sampler, "Christ is the Head of this House"? Suddenly there is a realization of the preciousness of the children or the recognition of the quiet growth and change in someone you see every day; the appreciation of how loyal that spouse has been, or a deep gratitude welling up to God for those you love; a remembrance that food and health are God's gifts to you. As these thoughts occur, life is being lived on two levels.

Master of the Storm

Read John 6:16–24

Comment: These facts stand out: the disciples had struck bad weather; Jesus came to them in the storm; in their fear they did not recognize him; he declared himself and assured them; at once they were safely at land.

Storms at sea struck terror in the Jews because they indicated disorder and chaos. As God's Spirit moved on the darkness of the waters at Creation bringing light and order (Gen. 1:2), so Jesus walked on stormy waters to bring peace and safe landing to his disciples.

John is telling us that when the waters of life seem to overwhelm us the risen Christ walks beside us, Master of wind and wave.

Reflection: A couple phoned me because their marriage was breaking up. They saw no hope. Could I help them? I panicked. Then I began to thank God that they wanted to see me. I felt at peace as they came. We talked of God and his love, of Christ and forgiveness. The miracle happened: two people found God and in doing so found each other. The floods of anger subsided. The facts of life were as before, but they were walking above the storm with the Christ. Their marriage was safely anchored.

Here are two responses to this personal storm: (1) The couple wanted out; they sought to separate themselves from life's buffetings; (2) I was afraid to counsel them until I felt the Presence of God within. When the waves of life threaten you what is your response? Tell how you have sensed the Presence of the Christ and how he is helping you to walk above the storms of life.

Hunger for Bread

Read John 6:25–40

Comment: Verses 26–27. Jesus wanted to lift the people from the level of mere earthly satisfactions of curiosity and physical appetites to a level of spiritual hunger for the food that endures forever.

Verses 28–29. In answer to the question, "What must we *do?*" Jesus said, *"Believe"!* But it was to be a quality of belief that would revolutionize the person's total thinking and acting.

Verses 30–38. They wanted another sign, not recognizing

that right there in the person of Jesus was the heavenly manna come alive and available for them. Now he spoke forthrightly, "I am the bread of life." He was not only the Bread-Giver in feeding the multitude, but he is himself the Bread and, like the manna, he also came down from heaven. To receive him, therefore, is to receive God's gift, the Bread of Life.

Verse 40. As physical food makes possible physical life, so Christ the Son offers eternal life to all who believe in him.

Reflection: In the light of verses 26 and 27 analyze your motives for going to church and for turning to God in prayer.

Verses 28–29. Do you ever busy yourself with activities to avoid this revolutionary experience of being confronted by the Christ? What does Jesus' command to *believe in him* mean to you?

Verse 35. Compare your hunger for meals, for TV news, for reports from your family and friends, for news about business or the stock market with your hunger for knowledge of and fellowship with Christ. How eager are you to partake of the Bread of Life?

Verses 37–39. Do you feel sure of your welcome when you come to God in prayer? When you come to Christ asking him to live within you? You are very special to him, you know, worth keeping through all eternity.

Verse 40 summarizes the theme of this Gospel (see also 20:30): John invites us to a quality of faith in the Son of God that gives an entirely new dimension to life. Life is now of the quality that will endure forever.

Feed on Him

Read John 6:41–71

Comment: Verses 54–56. The words, "He who eats my flesh and drinks my blood" would be abhorrent to both

Jew and Greek. But John carries the analogy relentlessly forward. There is an internalization about tasting and eating. The Psalmist wrote, "O taste and see that the Lord is good" (Ps. 34:8), and Ezekiel, "He said to me . . .'eat this scroll' . . . then I ate it, and it was in my mouth as sweet as honey" (Ezek. 3:1–3).

Furthermore, John wants these earthbound words—*wine, birth, water*—to be understood in terms of the Spirit. The wine we drink is the new wine of the Spirit; the birth we experience is from above; the water we drink is living water. In like manner the bread is none other than the Christ, who is himself Life and Food. The blood is Jesus himself offered up for us on the cross. The words, "He who eats my flesh and drinks my blood abides in me, and I in him," are a veiled reference to the Sacrament of the Lord's Supper.

These were difficult words to take. First, these religious authorities were literalists, incapable of thinking in spiritual terms. Bread was bread, flesh was flesh, blood was blood. They could not comprehend that his flesh was true food, that he was offering them something in the realm of the Spirit. Their thoughts and understanding were earthbound. Second, they saw Jesus himself in earthly terms—the son of Joseph and Mary (v. 42). They could not and would not see him as the One sent from God.

Verses 66–67. So they and many disciples turned away from Jesus. When he asked the twelve if they would leave him also, Peter replied with warmth and deep faith. No wonder Jesus loved him! Peter's statement here is parallel to his confession as recorded in Mark 8:27–30.

Reflection: With what do you satisfy the inner hungers of your life? With second-rate, substitutionary foods? Overeating, drinking, watching TV, titillating reading or fantasies, temper tantrums, criticizing others?

How do we cultivate this intimacy which is symbolized by eating Christ's flesh and drinking his blood? How do we cut through the limits of language to feel the power of faith? In the partaking of the Lord's Supper? The communion of silence? Seeing the light in a little child's eyes? Watching the sunrise? Sharing the agony of tortured Christians in foreign jails? Reading or listening to music? Sitting silently with one to whom the doctor has broken the news of terminal sickness? Sharing a needed dollar, a bit of food? Is it under a tall tree or beside a towering skyscraper? Is it in a meadow or on a city pavement where you have "tasted" the Christ?

There are four responses to Jesus' words here:

The religious legalists: Unable to see the Christ in Jesus. Unwilling to believe.

Many disciples: "A hard saying." The challenge was too much.

Peter and the few: "To whom shall we go? . . . we have believed."

Judas: Chose to betray him. Evil follows close on the heels of goodness.

Expand these responses in your mind. In what ways do you find yourself in them?

The Miracle of God's Timing

Read John: 7:1-13

Comment: Jesus' brothers wished to force his hand. They wanted him to prove his Messiahship if indeed he really were the Christ: "Is this brother of ours really who he claims to be?" (They did not believe in him, v. 5). Jesus made the reply, "The right time for me has not yet come, but any time is right for you" (NEB). God has his own timing for revealing himself and his works. Jesus was able to hold

45

back from a human desire to prove himself, to discomfort his enemies, to convince his family. He yielded to the restraining will of God.

Reflection: God's timing constantly amazes me. It is one of the great recurring miracles. Think of the difference between the pressure to prove oneself right, to win every battle, to force issues and unmask people; and the wisdom of letting matters ripen, sensing God's timing, and giving opportunity for the leavening work of the Holy Spirit.

Do you tend to vindicate your position and press for results? Such pressure can be counterproductive. Do you see yourself urging others to declare themselves and to take certain stands on issues before they are ready to do so of their own volition? Do you pressure yourself and thus fail to live with a leisurely fullness? Jesus lived with incomplete situations, as well as with "unfinished" people, and his heart was at peace. What is your record on waiting for God's timing as opposed to responding to human pressures, from yourself or another?

The Insights of Commitment
Read John 7:14–36

Comment: Verse 17. There is a wisdom that comes only from commitment and involvement. Recognition of God's will and a sense of personal identity come when we move out in faith to obey that which we believe to be God's will (see Heb. 11:8). Knowledge follows doing, but the reverse is not so often true.

Verses 19–36. These questions come to mind as we read these verses: How do we know that Jesus was the Christ? How do we establish our own self-identities? These are some of the clues: putting human values before religious traditions (vv. 21–23, which refer to the healing by the Pool,

5:2–10); a sense of mission or sentness (v. 28); a growing relation with God (v. 29); the bearing of fruit worthy of the heavenly Father ("signs," v. 31).

Jesus told his followers that he was to leave them physically and those who knew him only as a man from Nazareth would not see him again (vv. 27, 34). He was later to say that those who believed in him would receive him as a spiritual Presence who knew no time or space limitations. They would be with him forever (see 14:3).

Reflection: Verses 16–17. The question most frequently asked me at conferences is this: "How can I know the will of God?" It is significant that the question is invariably, "How can I *know?*" and not, "How can I *do?*" *Knowledge comes after doing.* How often we want to know first. In that case there would be no place for faith. God wants us to learn to trust that "hunch," that inner leading, "the soul's invincible surmise." We need to go out in faith, even though it involves making mistakes. Knowledge comes *with* doing. More appropriate questions would be, "What keeps me from doing God's will? Fear of failure? People's opinions? The unknown?"

Verses 22–23. How illogical we become as we try to uphold our beliefs and religious habits. I heard of a farmer apprehended by civil authorities for selling adulterated milk. He swore at the police. The church excommunicated him for swearing, but ignored his endangering the lives of children! Does your religion permit you to overlook human values and responsibilities to your community or neighbors?

Verses 27, 29. Do you box yourself in? How do you measure yourself? As your parents saw you: Clumsy? Lazy? Idolized? Loved? Affirmed? As others see you? As you alone see yourself? As God sees you? Are these different, as far as you know?

Signs and Controversies

I can see myself as someone coming from New England, a minister and teacher trying to gain confidence by successfully leading retreats, or I can have the confidence of being someone called of God to live and speak for him, empowered not by my skills but by his indwelling. God wants you to be a "sent" person called of him to be a student, a worker, a spouse, a parent, a teacher, a salesclerk, a very special child of his. As you respond to this call and accept an awareness of "sentness," the consciousness grows as to who *you really are*—born from above (3:3) and born of God (1:12, 13). Jesus had a strong sense of identity. He could answer the questions, "Who am I?" "Where have I come from?" "Why am I here?" What are *your* answers?

The Artesian Well

Read John 7:37–52

Comment: In a land of limited rainfall these words of thirsting and drinking would carry authority and hope for those who believed. To those who did not believe, this was nonsense. To have a sincere belief in Christ is to have an inner artesian well! This is Christ's promise (v. 38). Jesus uses figures of speech that reveal the inwardness and intimacy of his message. He does not advocate outward obedience to rules or fulfilling duties, no matter how praiseworthy they may be. He asks a relationship to himself that involves the indwelling of his spirit so that we may be led of his Spirit. This is followed by a joyous obedience to God's will.

Reflection: Verses 37–38. Jesus' words require a response from the depths of our being: a yes or a no. The source of power and of life itself is to be found through faith in Jesus Christ.

The crux of my own new birth in Christ forty-five years ago was the decision to let the Spirit of Christ enter into my inner life: my moods, imaginations, self-pityings, fantasies. I had argued that if I dedicated my outer life, my actions, to him I had the right to think my own thoughts and indulge in my own moods, whether withdrawn, judgmental, or self-centered. Then I was challenged to allow Christ to dwell in me so completely that the very springs of being deep within were from him. I decided to allow him to think his thoughts and to set in motion his moods and feelings through me. The ego within me was no longer to be me but Christ living in and through me (see Gal. 2:20).

The results were amazing. As I opened my heart in honesty I felt a cleansing, a freedom and an inrush of God's love and the love of my family. I felt a sense of healing as I became a whole and not a divided person. A crowded, frustrating program changed into an "ordered life" that confessed "the beauty of his peace." Instead of being a pressured strain, life had become an overflow from within.

Verses 40–52. Note the variety of responses! "He is the Christ." "No, just a prophet." "He cannot be anyone important. See where he was born!" "Let's seize him!" "No one ever spoke as he. . . . He is a wonderful man!" "This fickle multitude!" "The public be damned." And at long last, "Let's at least give him a fair hearing!" How do you respond?

Ponder the difference between acts that spring from duty and religious compulsion and those that are the spontaneous overflowing of Christ's indwelling love.

Sin Enveloped by Grace
Read John 7:53–8:11

Comment: Although the oldest and best manuscripts omit this story, it is worthy of comment because whether historical or not, it reflects the spirit of Jesus.

The Pharisees favored justice rather than mercy. The

keeping of the law superseded the worth of a woman; tradition overshadowed personhood.

Verses 6–8. The two occasions of Jesus' stooping and writing helped to erase Jesus as the focal point of the Pharisees' anger and brought them face to face with their own consciences. It was with their own thoughts they must wrestle. By stooping and looking at the ground, Jesus graciously avoided looking directly into the woman's eyes and spared her the necessity of any embarrassing return glance.

After the accusers left, Jesus directed the center of conversation from her sin to the vanishing accusers and revealed himself as the One who came, not to condemn, but to save (see 3:17). His command to "not sin again" was reinforced by his supportive behavior and his faith in her. The Pharisees, as is often the case with church people, sinned in the area of judgmentalism and condemnation. The woman's sins were those of appetite and passion. How easy to excuse the former by condemning the latter!

Reflection: Whenever I break the laws of God, or the laws that I have set for myself, invisible accusers point their fingers at me! My careless words may have hurt someone I love dearly; perhaps I have harbored resentful thoughts or I have overscheduled myself so that I cannot give of my best. The degree of my sinfulness is relatively unimportant. I stand accused whether for little or much. Persons are prone to measure the size of sins, but God does not. When I stand contrite in the presence of the Christ, the accusing fingers disappear and I am a person again hearing his words, "Do not sin again."

As a young boy learning to write I used a steel pen that I dipped in an ink well. Often as we made the upstroke of a letter the sharp pen point would catch in the rough paper and splatter a row of ink spots on our copy books. One day I had worked so carefully and the page was almost finished when—oops—the pen caught and there was a row of black spots. Try as I might to lean over my book and hide it, the teacher saw what had happened and without a word of scolding turned over the page and said lovingly, "Try again." Recall your encounters with sin, forgiveness and beginning again.

Contrast the attitudes of the Pharisees and of Jesus. On the one hand the Pharisees were critical, fault finding, looking for shortcomings in others, eager to mete out punishment, doubting human nature, protective of the traditions, strict constructionists. On the other hand, Jesus affirmed and appreciated the individual's personhood, looked for the good in others, had faith in human nature, was forgiving, redemptive, upbuilding.

On which level do you live? How do you rate yourself? Live through the scene again in your imagination. Note the exquisite sensitivity and graciousness of Jesus. What does it say to you?

The Light of the World

Read John 8:12–30

Comment: Verse 12. The Old Testament had said, "Thy word is a lamp to my feet and a light to my path" (Ps. 119:105). This light now became incarnate, enfleshed in Jesus as "The Light of the world." John, writing to Greek Christians, is saying that "light" is not to be found primarily in Greek wisdom nor in the Jewish Torah, but by belief in and obedience to him who was himself the Light. This Light does two things: exposes evil and makes good stand out. The pathway is plainly seen. The "light of life" brought new security to the journey.

Verses 13–15. Here was an impasse: The Pharisees from

cultured Judea could not see in Jesus anything but an unlettered Galilean carpenter. His unsupported words were suspect. They judged Jesus according to his human lineage; they saw him as a mere man.

Verses 16–29. Jesus said, in effect, "I have come from above. My whole outlook is of the Spirit. You are of the earth [v. 23], bound by your legalism and rules. You cannot understand me, you cannot live in this spirit of fellowship and freedom, because you do not recognize the Spirit of God in me."

Verse 30. Again people believed—this was the very purpose of John's writing this Gospel (20:31).

Reflection: Verse 12. What does the act of following Jesus imply for you? Describe the difference between walking in darkness and walking in the light of Christ as you have experienced it in your life. What has the light of Jesus meant to the pathways of your life? (See Col. 1:13, 14.)

Verse 19. Have you felt sometimes that your words or manner of life were like a foreign language to people around you, or that you even seemed almost crazy to them? How do you handle such an impasse? Can you keep communication open and continue in dialogue and encounter? Have you maligned or hurt another only to have that person forgive and love you? Has there come a moment of insight, of repentance and resolution which you can speak of as "knowing"?

Words of Righteous Indignation
Read John 8:31–47

Comment: This section carries more verbal hostility than any other part of the Gospel. The enmity against Jesus has been mounting through chapters 7 and 8. Jesus is in danger. We realize that from now on there will be growing and unreconcilable conflicts between the religious authorities and Jesus, ending in his death. The severity of Jesus' words about the Jews in verse 44 reminds us of his words in Matthew 23:23–33.

The Jews interpreted Jesus' words to refer to political freedom (v. 33). They thought that being descendants of Abraham gave them automatic status of freedom and privilege. They could not see that they were locked into their past and were slaves of tradition and of sin. Jesus was saying that freedom from the slavery of sin was the only true freedom.

Verses 41–47. The devil—Satan—is mentioned in verse 44 for the first time in this Gospel. He plays a more prominent role in the later chapters. By seeking to kill Jesus these religious leaders showed themselves to be children of the devil, who was a murderer and liar from of old. Jesus had said that these Jews did not behave like children of Abraham. Now the accusation was much more severe—they were not children of God, but of the devil. In 3:19–20 we read that children of darkness hate the light. Here the children of lying hate the truth. They would not see the truth in Jesus, but hated him and planned to kill him. Jesus was angry with the leaders because they had turned their backs on the truth and light that he embodied. His anger, however, did not spring from the context of hate, but of deep love. Therefore he was able to continue in encounter with them in righteous anger rather than with uncontrolled ill temper.

Reflection: Verses 31–40. Are there situations in which you are locked into your past? If you are a Republican do you find it more difficult to see good in a Democrat than in a fellow Republican—or vice versa? Does your being a "conservative" or "liberal" in politics or religion make it difficult for you to be free to see and evaluate clearly people with other viewpoints?

Because I had a demanding father, I came to think of God as a harsh, distant, exacting Deity. I was locked into fear. My view of God was warped. It was only when Jesus Christ with his boundless love entered my life that I was set free to see God as Jesus revealed him. I was freed from the slavery of fear to the warmth of love. Are there childhood imprisonments, cultural barriers, religious traditions that keep you from larger freedom in Christ?

Verses 41–47. Can you handle anger or does it master you? Can anger and love be for you opposite sides of the same coin? When our children were young I punished them for disobedience by whipping them. My wife would say to me after the punishment, "Now hold them in your arms while they are sobbing." But I would not do it. My anger had mastered me. What is your experience?

Sin had corrupted the perception of these leaders so that they could not and would not see the good in Jesus. They were of this world, "from below," and they could not recognize the God in Jesus who was "from above." Can you think of times when sin in the form of critical attitudes or envy kept you from seeing the good in some people? Contrast the evaluations you make of people when you are in fellowship with Christ and when you are out of fellowship.

Who Is This Man?

Read John 8:48–59

Comment: The Pharisees hoped to dispose of the issue by classifying Jesus as one of the despised group of Samaritans and calling him "demon possessed." Jesus' reply made him even more vulnerable: "If any one keeps my word, he will never taste death." The Jewish leaders could only see Jesus as a Galilean peasant. They did not sense his timeless

Spirit, the presence of the Eternal in him. To keep his word (vv. 52, 53) is to embrace his eternity and share with him a quality of life that is alive forevermore.

The Pharisees again referred to Abraham, comparing him to Jesus. Now Jesus witnessed to an even deeper truth, his warm relationship with God and his own eternal existence (v. 58). There is a profound depth to the words *I Am*. Jesus was proclaiming the depth of his being, a primeval oneness with God that was and is and ever will be (cf. the Gloria Patri). Note that each time Jesus was attacked he responded with a more outspoken witness which in turn was followed by increasing hatred and determination to kill him.

Reflection: Verse 48. The Jews lumped Jesus in with a hated group, the Samaritans. Recall times when you labeled a person in order to discredit him. "He's a Communist." "Oh, he's just a youngster, he doesn't know any better." "He's a newcomer around here." Why did you do this? How much easier for those leaders to say that Jesus "has a demon" than to listen and seek to understand! Are you willing to listen to and love those with whom you disagree?

Abraham is dated in history. Jesus as the Christ and Messiah is timeless and eternal. How do you find yourself responding to statements like these: "It seems as though I have always known Christ"; "Jesus puts me in touch with the endless sweep of God's love"; "Christ is mine and I am his forever"? What do Jesus' words "I am" say to you? This kind of reality also enters into human relationships: "It is as though we have *always* known each other." "Your love and friendship help me to be myself."

From Blindness to Sight

Read John 9:1–41

Comment: In this story everyone is blind. The blind man himself, the Pharisees who will not see (i.e., believe), the parents and the neighbors who fail to recognize Jesus as the Christ. The story ends with the blind man seeing both physically and spiritually as he believes in the Christ. Truly "the works of God [were] made manifest in him" (v. 3).

Once again there is a deeper meaning in this miracle of healing. The recording of the incident is not merely to tell of bringing eyesight to a blind man, but the announcement that Jesus is the Light of the world.

In verse 2 an age-old question is introduced: "Has this man's sin brought on his affliction or is he innocent?" Jesus bypasses the issue as irrelevant and focuses upon the works of God to be revealed through this man's healing. He then makes the dramatic announcement of being the Light of the world (see also 1:4, 9; 8:12).

The scene between the Pharisees and the healed man is one of spellbinding drama. The accusers stand accused: the lone man has born irrefutable witness, so in their hostility they use their authority to excommunicate him. The man whom the Pharisees thought to be ignorant and living in the darkness of sin (why else should he be born blind?) turns the tables on them. They were in the darkness of moral confusion and spiritual blindness: moral confusion because their keeping the Sabbath prevented them from showing mercy to one in need; spiritual blindness because their worship of Moses kept them from recognizing the acts of God in Jesus.

The climax of the story is found in the judgment that is meted out both to the Pharisees and the healed man. The Pharisees who believed they saw remained blind, for they did not recognize the Light when they saw it. The healed man, once physically blind, was now physically and spiritually sighted. He believed in Christ and therefore could see!

Reflection: Verses 2–3. For some suffering we are patently to blame. A little serious reflection or prayer will convince us of this. We can then repent, be forgiven, forgive ourselves, make whatever restitution God commands and begin a new way of life. But some sicknesses or accidents manifestly are not our fault. Let us stop asking questions like, "What have I done to deserve this?" and ask God to show us how this seeming tragedy can be turned into an "in-sight," asking for example, "Lord, what have you to show me or teach me through this? How can this be used as an opportunity for your purposes and blessings to be present in me?"

Think of situations in your life in which the blindness of prejudice kept you from seeing with wisdom and insight. I recall my resentment at my father's second marriage. It was several years before I could see the beauty and charisma in my stepmother's life. What have been your experiences?

Where are your areas of blindness? Seeking money and property as ends in themselves and not as opportunities for stewardship and service? Seeing a woman as an object of desire rather than a beautiful child of God to be gloried in? Seeing a job primarily as a means of advancement and not a situation in which to serve one's fellows? What new insights and enlightenments have come to you as the light of Christ has shone in your life?

Note the power of the witness of a changed life (vv. 15, 32). The man just told what happened. He did not argue. The Pharisees did the arguing and they lost! What does this say to you about the respective values of witness and argument when talking to others of your Christian experience?

Note the pilgrimage of the healed man: Physical blindness, encounter with Jesus, physical healing, admittance to religious circles where he is discredited by hypocritical leaders and excommunicated; then his second encounter with Jesus, spiritual healing, fulfillment in faith and worship. Do any of the above find a parallel in your life? In my own pilgrimage I recall being convicted, years ago, that my life was too self-centered. I made a new dedication to Christ. I found fellowship with some enthusiastic Christians who eventually disappointed me. This caused me to seek a deeper relationship with Christ, who has never ceased to open door after door into a more meaningful and rewarding life.

IV

The Shepherd and Giver of Life
(John 10:1–11:57)

Jesus as Door and Shepherd

Read John 10:1–21

Comment: Jesus recalled the familiar Old Testament theme of the Shepherd and the sheep (Ezek. 34; Ps. 23). He used two figures of speech, *door* and *shepherd*. He did not point to the door or seek to describe it. He did not define the qualities of the Good Shepherd. He stated simply and forthrightly that he personified both, embodying all that the Entrance to the fold or the Shepherd might be.

Jesus represented himself as both the gate (or door) to the sheepfold, traditionally a passive and feminine role, and also as Good Shepherd, an active and male image. In chapters 8 and 9 we see Jesus as the Giver of light and sight. In this chapter he is the Gateway to life and the Giver of life.

Verses 11–18. The Good Shepherd: the biblical definition of *good* is one who brings "blessings" and not "curses" (see Deut. 30:15–20). For John, the Good Shepherd leads his sheep from darkness and death to light and life. The mark of this kind of shepherd is his willingness to sacrifice himself for his sheep. There is a bond of love and fellowship—the shepherd knows his sheep and they know him. This bond is similar to the relationship of Christ and his church and between God and his Son (v. 15). This sacrifice is entirely voluntary on Jesus' part; it is performed in loving obedience to the Father's will.

The reaction of the Jewish leaders was violent. Their easiest solution was to say, "He has a demon." Yet a few who had witnessed the once-blind man running among them wild-eyed, gazing about and shouting, asked, "Can a demon open the eyes of the blind?" (v. 21).

Reflection: All of us are children of God. We are sheep of his fold, very precious to him. We are people for whom Jesus died and in whom God through the Risen Christ, the "great shepherd of the sheep," is forever at work (Heb. 13:20).

All of us are doors—people enter or fail to enter the Kingdom because of us. Parents are unconsciously presenting the image of the Heavenly Father to their children. People form their opinions of God from us. A door suggests the warm, inviting aspects of life. Do these characteristics need greater development in you?

All of us are shepherds. We are "under-shepherds" to the great Shepherd: pastors, parents, teachers, fellow workers in an office, store or factory, fellow members on committees, or members of a little neighborhood coffee klatch. All of these are little sheepfolds containing God's sheep. How do you define your role as shepherd in these groups?

Note the qualities Jesus includes in his description of the Shepherd: costly caring, courage, knowing the sheep, freedom and spontaneity of action. Here are both strong and tender qualities. A whole person, whether man or woman, embraces both the masculine and feminine aspects of personhood. Where do you see your strengths? Your weaknesses?

All of us at times are suspicious of innovators who threaten the status quo. How shall we judge new voices and by what standards shall we evaluate them?

Verse 18. "No one takes my life from me." Do you feel buffeted by life and robbed of your freedom? The risen Christ is yours that he may share with you his dignity and freedom.

I knew a man whose wife had died of cancer. A few days later he said to a few friends, "I did not choose to be a widower, to be a single parent of three small children, to sit at a table across from an empty chair. I did not choose all this for myself, but because this is the pathway that has opened for me and the way that God is calling me to go, therefore *I choose to live the life I did not choose."* The Christ who chose the cross is present within us so that we may choose to walk our difficult pathways with strength, with dignity and with freedom.

Jesus as Messiah and Son of God

Read John 10:22–42

Comment: Verses 24–38. The controversy is resumed from the close of chapter 9. The Pharisees asked him bluntly, "If you are the Christ, tell us plainly." Jesus' reply was fourfold: (1) I have told you. (2) The works I do bear witness to me. (*Works* is mentioned five times in this passage.) (3) You are not my sheep by your own exclusion, so of course you cannot believe. (4) My Father and I are one . . . He in me and I in him. And he says even more plainly in verse 37, "I am the Son of God."

The Shepherd and Giver of Life

We learn in this passage who the Messiah really is: "He is the Son who being one with the Father is the Giver of eternal life" (Dodd, *The Interpretation of the Fourth Gospel*, p. 361). This is the first time that Jesus' claim is both public and explicit.

Verses 39–42. They tried to arrest him, but he recognized that it was not God's time for his sacrifice, and so eluded their grasp. He returned to the place of his baptism; the author once more connects John the Baptist's ministry with that of Jesus. Again the familiar refrain, "many believed."

Reflection: (a) What is your response to Jesus' words, "I told you, and you do not believe" (v. 25)? Which of all the recorded *words* of Jesus has meant the most to you? Caused the greatest change in your lifestyle? Fostered the greatest growth? Have some words of Jesus been difficult for you to believe? Why?

(b) Ask yourself the same questions as in the preceding paragraph, substituting the word *works* for *words*.

(c) What does it mean to you to be one of Jesus' sheep? Note the promises of verse 28: *eternal life*—a way of life that breathes of wholeness and purpose; a sense of the worthwhileness of the battle; always light at the end of the tunnel. *Never to perish*—we are not made merely for earth, we are being fashioned for eternity. Each day is a day of learning in a process of never-ending growth and adventure. *Security*—"No one shall snatch them out of my hand." Here is a place to rest and hide! We are "tucked in God's overcoat pocket." But it is also a launching pad, a place in which to make decisions and from which to act. What is happening in your life as you make these three gifts in verse 28 your own (eternal life, never to perish, security)?

(d) Note the relationship of God and Jesus as described

in verses 30 and 38. Does this change your idea of God? Make him more understanding? Caring? Available? Approachable? What effect does it have on your idea of Jesus? The authority of his words? As an authentic guide for life? As the Author of light and life for our lives? Reflect on this union of God and Jesus and how, through this union, they affect your life in new ways.

Willingness is always a prerequisite to being a sheep in Jesus' fold. Sometimes when my wife has temporarily lost the joy of living, I ask her if she has prayed about it and she replies, "That's the trouble; I don't want to pray about it. If I wanted to pray, everything would be all right." We cannot always will to love, but we can will to pray, to listen to God and to be obedient. The key word is *willingness.* Then the miracle of love and inclusion breaks through.

The theme of chapter 11 is Christ revealed to us as Resurrection and Life. In verses 1–16 we see him going to face death— death in Lazarus and also moving closer to his own death. In the body of the chapter (vv. 17–44) we have the raising of Lazarus and the conversation with the sisters. In both situations Jesus stood revealed as Resurrection and Life. The conclusion (vv. 45–57) depicts the events hastening toward Jesus' death and the irony of the leaders seeking to kill him who is Resurrection and Life! The raising of Lazarus is the last sign to be included in this Gospel before the Passion Story which begins at the end of chapter 11. So at the conclusion of his ministry we see Jesus as Victor over death, but moving to his own death which in turn ends in victorious life. Jesus' death and resurrection comprised the greatest sign of all, climaxing all that had taken place before.

Living and Dying to the Glory of God
Read John 11:1–16

Comment: Verses 1–5 set the stage and give us a feeling of the warm fellowship Jesus had with that family. The story of the anointing of Jesus' feet is told in the next chapter (12:3). John assumed all his readers would know of the incident. The final word is not death but the glory of God, and this glory God shares with his Son.

Verses 6–16. This dialogue between Jesus and his disciples took place beyond the Jordan (see 10:40). Here, Jesus moved toward his own death while on an errand to conquer death! Again the accent in verse 15, "that you may believe"—this time that Jesus as the Son of God is Resurrection and Life. It is quite evident in verse 16 that the disciples were all convinced the religious authorities would kill Jesus, and that they, the disciples, would die with him.

Reflection: Verse 4. How have sicknesses, in your experience, been used for the glory of God? When has illness not honored God? What factors caused this?

Think of emotional sicknesses that are "unto death": "I'm sick of everything; I'd like to jump in the river." "I'd like to end it all." "Life has lost its meaning for me." It is in these crises as well as in physical sickness that this Christ comes with his gift of life.

Verse 6. A sentimental friend would have rushed to Lazarus's bedside at once. Jesus waited for God's timing. How often I have rushed to minister to sick people, thinking that I was so necessary to their welfare. I am a typical "yes man," but I am slowly learning to wait and not rush in before God's Spirit has had time to do his work.

Verses 7–16. Consider the thought of moving toward death, physical or emotional, to bring about life: a mother in childbirth, or a person befriending an unwanted or unpopular person in a group or community.

Are you being called to go through "valleys of death" or into difficult or dangerous situations in order to bring newness of life? How are you responding?

Life Meets Death

Read John 11:17–44

Comment: "In the midst of life we are in death." So reads the funeral service in the Book of Common Prayer. Jesus has come to Bethany so that in the midst of death they may be in life! Christ brings a "reversal to the order of mortality." Life in Christ is no longer hastening toward death, but death is moving toward life.

Verses 21–32. "If you had been here!" The sisters utter identical words. They must have said them over and over as they waited for Jesus to come. Martha believes in the general resurrection at the last day. Jesus is saying, in effect, "Not only is that resurrection awaiting you, but here and now the resurrection is present, for I am both Resurrection and Life." Martha reaches out in faith to believe this.

Verses 33, 35, 38. How deeply involved Jesus was! He was no professional dealing with a situation at arm's length! This was a costly encounter for Jesus. Bishop John V. Taylor in *The Go Between God* speaks of three stages in the work of the Holy Spirit in us: *awareness, responsibility* and *sacrifice.* How graphically these steps are portrayed here in Jesus!

Verses 40–41. In the very presence of death, Jesus spoke of the glory of God. Jesus' prayer was not one of petition that the miracle would take place. His faith in his Father's love and power was so sure that he thanked God *in advance* for the mighty deed that was about to take place. It was a reality in the heart of God before it became an event on earth.

Verses 43–44. Jesus challenged the grave. Life gave its victory shout over death. Jesus commanded the man to help himself at Bethzatha (5:8); here he asked Lazarus's friends to "Unbind him, and let him go."

Reflection: Verse 21. "If you had been here." He is *always* "here," often unseen that our faith may be strengthened, and ready to reveal himself in power at the crucial moment.

Verse 25. The living Christ offers to each of us his own Being. Into our little "I ams" (the beings that we are) he enters with his own being, his "I AM." He speaks to us through the years: At our birth and rebirths he says, "I am Life"; in the uncertain years, "I am Shepherd"; when we are lost, "I am the Way"; amid changing morals and codes, "I am the Truth"; when faint, "I am food and drink"; when lost in dark confusion, "I am Light"; when dead in sin, "I am new birth"; when bored, "I am new wine"; when dying, "I am resurrection."

Verse 41. Jesus' prayer was in the past tense. It was a *prayer of affirmation* thanking God in advance that it had already happened! God had heard and answered the prayer. This kind of praying claims the future as having already happened, so that we can live in joy and confidence because we have faith in the ultimate victorious outcome.

Try a thirty-day experiment: *Stop asking God for anything.* Instead of the prayer of petition use the prayer of affirmation. (Note: The prayer of petition is not wrong. Jesus used it frequently. But we get in the habit of using it exclusively and so are robbed of the joy and power of the prayer of affirmation.) Instead of asking God to protect or guide your loved ones, affirm that it is so. Instead of asking God to heal you or others when sick, thank him that he is already doing it. To learn to pray with affirmation, start your prayers in some such way as, "God, I thank you that . . ." or "My Father, I rejoice that . . ."

The story of Lazarus is included as the climactic sign for three reasons: that we may know that the Christ who is Resurrection and Life is with us in the crucial death and dying situations of life even as he was with Lazarus; that we may receive newness of life and power as we believe in this Christ; that we may look forward with faith to the final resurrection when all who have died in Christ will rise to live with him in his glory.

The Inevitable Encounter with Christ
Read John 11:45–57

Comment: Verses 45–50. Again the refrain, "believed in him"! The plot to kill Jesus was well advanced. Now it was only a matter of days. The religious leaders feared political repercussions from Jesus' acts. What irony that Caiaphas uses the very words in verse 50 that most accurately describe Jesus' mission! One man to die that a whole nation should not perish—it reminds us of John 3:16!

God uses the schemes of the wicked as well as the obedience of his children. Joseph said to his brothers, "You meant evil against me; but God meant it for good, to bring it about that many people should be kept alive, as they are today" (Gen. 50:20). In like manner God used the evil of the religious leaders for good to bring countless people into newness of life in Christ as they are in his church today.

Verse 54. Once again as in 10:39–40 Jesus withdrew. He was waiting for "his hour," God's hour!

Verses 55–57. There were varied opinions. The curious wanted to see another miracle; those healed or blessed were filled with gratitude; many were puzzled; some hoped he might be the long expected Messiah; and some actively feared or hated him and sought to kill him.

Reflection: Verses 45–46. "Many . . . believed . . . but some." John makes constant reference in this Gospel to "believing in him." Belief in Christ, for me personally, is to take him as my Savior and Lord. The blind man experienced Jesus as Savior when he received his sight and as Lord when he obeyed Jesus' command, "Go and sin no more."

Forty years ago after four nervous breakdowns and three months in a sanitarium I turned in desperation to Christ as my only hope. I came; I yielded; I found Peace. He was—and is—my Savior. From then on I have sought to obey him. He has become my Lord, my King, my Messiah, forever. This is both an accomplished fact and a continuing process, a daily lifestyle.

Every time we encounter Jesus Christ we are faced with decision: to believe or not to believe; to obey or disobey; to follow or to desert. What have been your responses in some of the situations where this Christ has confronted you?

Verse 48. What considerations enter into your decision making? Remaining on the popular side? Threatened security? The desire for power? Desire to serve? Or, as so often with me, plain selfishness and inertia?

Verses 49–50. Caiaphas twisted a sacred truth to serve selfish ends. How easily we slip into this! "This is Sunday, a day for quiet. Can't you kids shut up so I can sleep?" "I'd like to help that cause, but I'm giving to my church." "What will happen to our churches if those foreigners move into town?" Does this strike home?

Verse 52. "To gather into one the children of God who

are scattered"—a beautiful picture of the Church. What have been some of your experiences of gathering and healing scattered and estranged people?

The focus of chapter 12 is the foreshadowing of Jesus' death and resurrection: the anointing of Jesus in preparation for burial; the Triumphal Entry symbolic of the risen King riding in victory; the seed falling into the earth, dying and bearing its fruit; Jesus lifted up and drawing all men to him; the Light of the World, in the world only a short time, bearer of the promise of eternal life.

V

Close of the Public Ministry
(John 12:1–50)

The Prodigality of Gratitude

Read John 12:1–11

Comment: Verses 1–8. There was eating and celebration in spite of the fact that both Jesus and Lazarus were marked for killing. Martha and Mary were true to their respective roles: Martha the worker; Mary the worshiper. Mary's devotion knew no bounds. It denied all practical ethics. After Judas' response, he is described as a thief, John's Gospel alone saying this. Verse 7 is difficult. What is the "it"? If it is the ointment, it has already been used. It could be "let her keep the memory," i.e., "Do not spoil the memory of what she has done."

Verse 9. The presence of the great crowd fanned the flames of envy so that the chief priests wanted to include Lazarus also in their lethal designs.

Reflection: Place yourself in a situation parallel to that of Jesus. You and a friend are being slandered, unkindly treated. Perhaps an act of friendship has been distorted and used against you. The disparager is a friend of yours, unable to perceive your interest. He is almost a traitor! Could you eat with him, carry on with poise and goodwill, speaking firmly but not peevishly? Have you been in a situation like this?

Put yourself in Mary's place. She is overcome with gratitude because of her brother's return to life (11:43, 44). Is there a place in love and devotion for extravagance? Here is a feeling act that knows no limits or reason. What moral claims do the needs of others make on us? Should she have been more disciplined in this costly expenditure? What are some of your ways of showing gratitude? Are they in keeping with society's needs around you?

In contrast to Mary's outgoing love is Judas's miserly withholding. Is he *all* bad? Put yourself, in turn, in the place of Jesus, Mary, Martha, Lazarus, Judas, an onlooker. What are your responses?

Blessed Is He that Comes in the Name of the Lord
Read John 12:12–19

Comment: All four Gospels are written with the wisdom of hindsight. Everything in Jesus' life is viewed through the filters of the resurrection and the life of the Church. At the time that it happened, the meaning of this victory ride was not clear to the disciples (v. 16). Only after the death-resurrection event when Jesus was glorified did they perceive Palm Sunday as the triumphal entry of the King.

Verse 19. Note the ironic statement, so skillfully worded, put in the mouths of the Pharisees. The opposition of Jesus' enemies served to intensify the witness for the Christ.

Reflection: Could you "ride in triumph" when only six days away from death? Recently I was at a retreat when a woman in her forties said her doctor had told her that she had an inoperable cancer. Her case was terminal. He prescribed intensive chemotherapy. She told us that she was claiming healing and victory in Christ. Her eyes were radiant. Her husband and she were growing in closeness and tenderness to each other. No one in that retreat ministered to us as did they. Here was a "triumphal ride." Whether or not she died in the flesh was completely overshadowed by the confidence that, living or dying, they were victorious and God was "glorified"—honored—by their manner of living.

List five triumphs in your life. What does your list reveal to you?

We Wish to See Jesus

Read John 12:20–36

Comment: Jesus' mission was to the Jews, i.e., to his own people. They turned against him. After his death-resurrection he would draw *all* men to him (v. 32) and his mission would be widened. There would be other sheep to be gathered into the fold (see John 10:16). John wrote his Gospel for Greek Christians. It is significant therefore that John recounts at the close of Jesus' ministry, this band of Greeks sought him out. Because they were coming to the Passover, they were evidently Jews with Grecian culture. It would appear that Jesus did not see them personally, but he spoke to their situation. He said, in effect, "The time of my exaltation is at hand. It will come about through my death. As a grain of wheat by dying bears much fruit, so my death will bring an abundant harvest. The door will be opened to Gentiles and they will be drawn to me" (v. 23).

Jesus had frequently used the word *glorified*. It occurs in two verses in this passage, 23 and 28. *Glorify* signifies to honor, to exalt. Jesus' prime purpose on earth was to glorify or honor God. This is a recurring theme in the Gospel: Jesus came from God (from above), lived in the flesh, modeled the love of God, was crucified, raised and returned to God, thus honoring his Father.

Verse 32. There is a play on words and a little subtle irony in Jesus' being "lifted up." He is lifted up from the earth by his enemies, nailed to a cross, thereby making for greater visibility. But by his willingness to be thus physically lifted up, he is eternally lifted up to a place of glory and honor with God, to be eternally visible and available to us as Savior and Giver of life (see 3:14, 15).

Reflection: Verse 21. Years ago I was preaching in a church in Rochester, New York. Carved on the back of the pulpit were five words visible only to the preacher: "Sir, we would see Jesus." I wrote the sentence on a little card, tucked it in my pocket and read it from time to time. What a sentence with which to begin a day, with which to set one's attitude for a task!

Verse 22. In the light of the comment above on *glorify,* in what ways does your life honor God?

Verse 26. Serving and following imply obedience. We often overlook Jesus' implicit obedience of his Father. Jesus expects us likewise to be obedient, then God will honor (or glorify) us. If you love God and are seeking to obey him, it is his desire to honor you. Do you believe God honors (exalts, glorifies) you? If not, what does it say about your self-image?

Verse 27. Here we see the humanity of Jesus. He was tempted as we are. He dreaded, he feared, he wanted out! But he did not give in to temptation. He saw that the Calvary road was the Glory road. The thing he feared became the gateway to accomplishing his mission in life. Recount instances when you have dreaded some situation but, when you went forward and faced it, you walked on your Glory road.

Verse 28. How often God reassures us while we are on the road. In the darkest night a light shines, a voice speaks, a friend is suddenly near.

Verse 35–36. Here is the dividing line: the Old Testament speaks of blessings and curses as the reward for obedience and disobedience, respectively (Deut. 30:19). Matthew separates the sheep from the goats (Matt. 25:32). John says that we will either be children of the light or walk in darkness. How do you perceive light and darkness at work in your life?

The Postscript

Read John 12:37–50

Comment: This section marks the close of the ministry of Jesus and leads us into the Passion Story (chaps. 13 ff.).

Verses 37–43. Here we have John's own comment and evaluation. He laments, "They did not believe in him" (see also 1:11). He quotes two passages from Isaiah which speak of rejection. However, he corrects his sweeping statement of verse 37 and says, "nevertheless many even of the authorities believed," though secretly.

Verses 44–50. These verses serve as postscript and summarize the main themes that have been stressed in chapters 2 through 12: Jesus sent by God as Light and Judgment; Jesus' obedience to and oneness with his Father; Jesus as Life. The "last day" is already present, because the Son of God who will be the Judge at the last is now present among them. By refusing to believe they are already judged; by refusing to walk in the light of Christ, they have condemned themselves to walk in darkness.

Reflection: Verses 42–43. Nicodemus was one of these "authorities." Compare his willingness to take a stand (7:50–52; 19:39), as over against those leaders who depended on human approval. Where do you place yourself in relation to these?

Christ is here with us today as truly as he was present then. Do you feel his Presence as Light and Life, Shepherd and Judge?

Does Christ appear to you mostly in a condemning or an affirming role? Are you comfortable or uncomfortable in his presence? What is this saying to you?

Chapters 13 through 17 comprise the final acts and the farewell conversations of Jesus before his actual death. The dramatic scenes at the Last Supper (13:1–30) foreshadow his death. The discourses (13:31–17:26), however, describe the new life that is offered to Christians after Christ's death, resurrection and exaltation. John represents Jesus as actually speaking the words before his death, but they are spoken from the vantage point of faith wherein the risen Christ is abiding in and living through his disciples and the Church. Throughout chapters 1 through 12 *life* and *light* have been the key words. In chapters 13 through 17 these two words are caught up in the deeper reality of *love:* love between the Father and the Son, among the Son and his disciples, and among all of Christ's disciples as the Church.

VI

The Last Supper
(John 13:1–30)

Serving but Not Servile

Read John 13:1–17

Comment: Verses 1–3. There is a majestic sweep in verses 1 and 3. Jesus was to return to his Father. He had accomplished his mission of love. He knew whence he came and where he was going. He was aware of the tremendous responsibility he carried: "His hour had come" . . . "all things in his hands." Yet ominously Evil entered into the very center of this sublimity. Furtively Judas was planning betrayal!

Verses 4–5. Following the superb introduction we read, "He girded himself with a towel . . . and began to wash the disciples' feet." Although King and Messiah he humbled himself to do the task of a slave. The lowly act of washing feet anticipated the humiliation of the cross. At first thought this seems a terrible letdown until we realize that this parallels and symbolizes the death-resurrection sequence again. Just as the grain of wheat dies to bear much fruit, so Jesus laid down his Kingship to win regal authority through the ages. Paul writes of this humiliation and exaltation in Philippians 2:5–11.

Verses 6–8. Peter could not comprehend Jesus' act of self-humbling any more than he could comprehend later that night the meaning of Jesus' arrest. He resisted both and did not see them as a necessary part of the death-resurrection path which Jesus had chosen to follow.

Reflection: Verses 1–3. Consider the entrance of the demonic into the most intimate and casual situations. Have vagrant, even downright mean thoughts, come to you at otherwise beautiful moments? How do you handle them? Jesus got into action at once, *self-humbling* action!

Verses 9–17. "If I do not wash you, you have no part in me." This is a veiled reference to the necessity for baptism. But it speaks more deeply of our need to be humbled before Christ. His acts of self-humbling, such as coming to earth in human form, washing the disciples' feet, and giving of himself to be crucified, demand on our part a parallel humility. To receive a menial service from a slave could well increase one's pride and indifference, but to receive such an act from a King whom we honor demands our brokenness and humiliation.

I recall a good Scottish friend of mine who often said, "I dinna want to be beholden to anyone." This is in direct contrast to Jesus who was dependent on his Father and who asks us in turn to be dependent on him. Once we yield and let the Master start to cleanse us, we find ourselves saying with Peter, "Lord, cleanse my whole being." I find in myself a recurring need to be cleansed by Christ. Sometimes I am too stubborn to come to him. How patiently he waits until I am ready! Recall when you have felt like saying with Peter, "Not my feet only . . ." In other words, "Lord, make it total!"

When people want to serve or wait on you are you reluctant to receive their offers? Jesus not only gave freely, but received freely (see 12:3–8). What keeps you from receiving freely?

Finally, we are under command to wash one another's feet (v. 14). Some churches take this literally. I shall never forget how deeply moved I was to see a Mennonite wash and anoint a brother minister's feet. Most of us take the command symbolically, but we still can take it seriously. We are called to be servants one of another, serving without being servile, humble without being humiliated. If our service, no matter how menial, is done at Christ's bidding and in his spirit, it is done with dignity and joy. Reflect on whether you undertake or avoid menial tasks; on how you feel when you are doing them; on how joyous you think Jesus must have felt. Do you believe that you have the right to the same kind of joyous feeling that he had? Is this what Jesus meant when he said, *"Blessed* [lit. *happy*] are you if you do them"?

It Was Night

Read John 13:18–30

Comment: Verse 30. "And it was night." The stark simplicity of the words brings a chill to the reader. John meant more than a time period. It was night in Judas's heart. He refused to walk in the light of Jesus and went out into the darkness of self-will and sin. It was night in the lives of the disciples. One of their number was betraying their beloved Master; they began to realize that the death he foretold was imminent. It was night for Jesus. He was soon to be crying out, "My God, my God, why have you forsaken me?"

Reflection: Role play the people at the supper table. See if you share any of their motives, fears or hopes. If you do, what would you like to do about them?

Judas: Does Jesus know? Do the disciples suspect? It won't be too bad; the Master will extricate himself. The thirty pieces of silver will look good. I'll put some of it in the bag so the others can share in it. Why did I ever become involved? His ideas are too visionary anyway.

A disciple: Could it be I? I know I've quarreled, wanted to be the leader. I've doubted the Master again and again—but betray him? Never! But is doubting him, refusing to follow him, the same as betraying him?

Jesus: My God, I knew I had to suffer and die, but did my betrayal have to come from one of my own? Judas! How often I have prayed for you and hoped that you would be faithful. I had great dreams for you. My Father, must I let my last act be one of love for him? Dip in the dish with him? Yes, Father, I'll do it. I accept my death and resurrection as your will for me.

The events around that table happen to all of us. In a sense every meal is our *last* meal; we shall not pass this way again. Betrayal is on every hand: we make war in the name of the Christ who would not kill but gave himself to be killed; we spend money in self-defeating luxuries while millions starve and minorities receive inferior education; we "sell" our friends for a morsel of gossip; we treat non-family with respect, but our family gets the brunt of our fury; we accept God's gifts greedily, but have little time for him.

Verse 30. It was night for both Judas and Jesus: endless night for Judas, but for Jesus a night that became eternal day.

VII

The Farewell Discourse
(John 13:31–16:33)

Will You Lay Down Your Life for Me?

Read John 13:31–38

Comment: Verses 31–32. Jesus by faith saw beyond the suffering on the cross and death to the triumph of the resurrection, and therefore spoke of himself as glorified. He lived as though the future had already happened!

Verses 34–35. This is the end result toward which the Gospel has been moving. It started with God's love mediated to us through Jesus. Now we are to love one another as he loved us. *Christians' loving one another is the authentic witness to the world.*

Verses 36–38. The Jewish leaders could not follow Jesus because they were unwilling to believe in him. The disciples could not follow because they were not prepared, not sufficiently disciplined. Peter's denial was evidence of this. But the time will come ("you shall follow afterward") when they will follow him and be true to the death.

Reflection: Verses 31–32. Cite an experience when in the midst of suffering or betrayal you have been able to rejoice because of your confidence in the outcome.

Verses 34–35. Is love the central fact of life for you? As a teacher do you believe that your love for your pupils is of first importance? As a parent for your children? As an employer for your workers? As a worker for your fellow workers and boss? What would happen if Jesus' quality of love motivated and directed you? What kind of a witness would this lifestyle make to the world?

Verses 36–38. "You shall follow afterward." Jesus had unending faith that Peter was redeemable. What is your attitude toward people that you cannot depend on? Do you still believe in such people? Do you feel Jesus believes in you regardless of how often you fail? He does, you know! How do you feel about that?

Do we ever say, "You've got to prove yourself trustworthy and then I'll trust you"? This amazing Jesus, trusting untrustworthy disciples! Their very hope of becoming trustworthy was Jesus' continuing faith in them.

Do you ever go overboard expressing your loyalty only to fail ignominiously soon afterward? I promise my wife to be home on time to receive some expected company, or I promise God to keep my thoughts Christ-centered, and how often I fail! Yet God still believes in me and loves me. Is there any of the Peter in you?

The die is cast. The Sanhedrin (the ruling body of the Jews) has voted to kill Jesus. Judas has gone out to betray him. There is no turning back.

From now on (13:31–17:26) John records Jesus as speaking with the perspective of hindsight as if the glorification (the death and resurrection) had already happened. Theologically, this is known as "realized eschatology"; that is, seeing the final end of things in the present tense. In the mind of Jesus, through faith, the crucifixion and resurrection are accomplished facts. "The Son of Man *is* glorified" (13:31).

Chapters 14 and 15 are the completion of John 3:16. The Gospel starts with the great love of God coming "from above" to us through his Son Jesus. It is through him we have salvation and enter into life. This life was to be realized through faith in a physically present Jesus, but after the crucifixion it is realized through the indwelling presence of God and his eternal Son (14:23). The Jesus of history located in space and time (Palestine, c. 4 B.C.–A.D. 29) has now become the Christ of experience, who dwells in us forever, regardless of place or time.

A Basis of Hope and Confidence

Read John 14:1–14

Comment: Verse 1 says in effect, "Don't be troubled because I am going away. As loyal Jews you believe in God; put the same faith in me, for I have come from God."

Verses 2–3. This is one of the most specific references in the Bible to the heavenly home. "Many rooms" implies there is room for all. Jesus goes there by way of his death and resurrection. It was a homecoming for him, but he will return to dwell within us so that we too can imitate his obedience to the will of God, die to self and enter into the life of the resurrection.

Verses 5–6. Thomas was puzzled about the way. Jesus replied that he, Jesus, embodied "the real and living way" (Moffatt).

Verses 7–11. Jesus had told the disciples repeatedly, but still they could not recognize that God was incarnate in Jesus and to know him as Christ was to know and see God. It was the aim of Jesus to glorify and honor his Father;

whoever believed in Jesus as the Son of God would be one with him in this purpose. Jesus was leaving and could no longer honor his Father on earth, but he left that task to all who believed in him. He promised unlimited support for their faith ("He who believes in me," v. 12) and answers to their prayers ("whatever you ask in my name," v. 13).

Reflection: Reread 13:1–3 and then 14:1–3. Here is a Person who lived with confidence. He knew where he was going and that his Father would honor him. This Jesus as the living Christ is *to be with you.* What does this say about your resting confidently in him? Walking tall in this faith? Facing any kind of future unafraid? Jesus is saying, "Trust me as you face life's traumatic situations, or even death. I know all about where you are going. I am going on ahead of you and when you enter into your new circumstances I will be with you."

Verses 4–7. Do you find yourself longing for a road map of life detailing each turn of the road? If you had it, what need then for faith? What place for surprise?

Verses 8–11. Jesus came to show us his Father and assure us that to see one was to see the other. Because of the warmth and love in Jesus, we can assume this to be God's nature. Do you feel a sense of awe toward both God and Jesus, for with them is majesty and judgment? Are you also conscious of their steadfast, tender caring? Thus you combine a feeling of both fear and love toward God.

Verses 12–14. Where is our emphasis when we ask God for things? Is it not frequently on the things asked for? On security? Healing? Deliverance from trouble? The thrust of these verses is not that God will do anything and everything we ask, but that everything done should bring honor to Christ. Our main concern should not be the granting of our requests, but the honoring of God and Christ. In what way would this change your way of praying? For me, on one occasion, it caused me to stop asking God to heal my pneumonia and to ask him so to increase my faith in Christ that this sickness might be to his glory. The pneumonia left in due time, but the entire sickness proved to be a rich benediction and a time of empowerment.

The Gift of Peace

Read John 14:15–31

Comment: Verse 15. Love and obedience characterized Jesus' attitude toward his Father. He therefore asks the same response from us.

Verses 16–17. This is the first of five sections in chapters 14 through 16 that deal with the promise of the Holy Spirit (14:16–17, 25–26; 15:26–27; 16:4b–11, 12–15).

Verses 16–17. The Holy Spirit is referred to as the Counselor and the Spirit of truth. *Counselor* is variously translated "Advocate," "Comforter" and "Helper." Jesus' stay was temporary. The Counselor was to be with them forever.

Verse 20. "In that day" is both at the final resurrection as well as in the here and now as the risen Christ dwells in our lives. Here is a triple relationship. Jesus in God, his disciples in Jesus, and Jesus in his disciples.

Verses 21–22. As in verse 15 obedience and love are joined together. Loving obedience opens the way for discernment to recognize Jesus as he manifests himself to us. Christ is seen only by those who love and obey him.

Verse 23. Here is an extraordinary statement: the Father of Jesus loves us and together with Christ will come and make his home in us. What an event to celebrate! Note once again the condition: love and obedience!

Verses 25–26. The second promise of the Spirit. Here the Counselor is also called the Holy Spirit and his function is that of Teacher. There will be constant refreshment as the words of Jesus are recalled.

Verse 27. Christ's peace is a gift, a legacy, bequeathed to those who live in him. The world, not knowing Christ, cannot receive his peace.

Verse 28. Their love could easily be a possessive love that wanted to hold on to Jesus (note Mary's clinging in the garden, 20:17). A generous love on their part would rejoice in Jesus' prospective homecoming to his Father. "Greater than I": God is the one who sent Jesus and whom Jesus obeyed, but they were one in spirit and fellowship.

Verse 30. Evil is always at work in the world, but Jesus had won this victory in advance. He had faced victoriously Peter's coming denial (13:38), Judas' betrayal (13:27), and his approaching death (12:23, 13:1). Hence Satan had no hold on him.

Verse 31. Again we see the love and obedience toward his Father. The final words are like a shout of victory! He knew what lay ahead and with a rallying cry called on his disciples to go forward with him. It is not necessarily a change of physical location, but the expression of a victorious attitude.

Reflection: Verse 15. Love can be sentimental and possessive with little obedience. Obedience can be duty-bound, uninteresting and loveless. What are the respective places of love and obedience in your life?

Verses 16–17. This Counselor is a friend forever! Often he is with us and we do not recognize him. Those hunches, those leadings, those thoughts like "Why didn't I do that when it first occurred to me?" are evidences that the Counselor is already at work in your life.

Verses 18–20. Christ offers us friendship and life, secured by this triple relationship (see *Comment*).

Verse 21. Reflect on the deepening of your love for Christ, first as it is disciplined by your obedience and then enriched beyond measure by his love for you and revelation of himself to you.

Verse 23. This verse is one of my favorites! The God who so loved us that he gave us his Son (3:16) wants with this Son to make his home in me and in you. Loving obedience and faithful acceptance are the keys. Does this verse grip you deeply, too?

Verses 25–26. The Holy Spirit speaks to us in the contemporary scene. Recount some incursions of the Spirit into your life, beckonings to new ways of living.

Verse 27. I find I need to practice the art of receiving the gift of peace. I often rush into tasks and plow through difficulties. I often work under tension. I am learning to relax, receive the gift of peace and then obediently and calmly go forward.

Verses 30–31. One of the secrets of Christ's strength was his strategy of winning the victory before the battle! He met crises victoriously in advance: eating a Festival meal with those who would desert him, washing the feet of one who would deny him, dipping in the dish with one who would betray him. What is your strategy for winning battles in advance?

As his disciples and as members of his Church, Christ is calling us to share in his victory here on earth and in the ultimate triumph of the life to come.

The Allegory of the Vine
Read John 15:1–17

Comment: Once again in this chapter it is the crucified and risen Christ who speaks to us. He has previously spoken of the intimate relationship of himself and his disciples with the symbolic language of drinking his blood and eating his flesh (6:54–56). Now he uses the allegory of the vine to illustrate the mystical union between himself and his friends. We renew this union as we drink from the cup at Communion. As branches abide in the vine, so the disciples abide in him. The branches are part of and dependent upon the Vine which in turn supplies them with their very life and potential to bear fruit. Verse 5 speaks of life with Christ, verse 6 of death without Christ. As we have discovered, life and death are major themes in this Gospel.

Verses 7–11. Three things result from this abiding in Christ: (1) A new quality of prayer life. (2) The honoring of God by the fruitfulness of his people. (3) Overflowing joy. He gave them peace (14:27); now he gives them joy! Jesus has loved us with the very love of God. To abide in Christ is to abide also in this great love of God.

Verses 12–17. These verses describe the community of faith, the Church that is to be. Love is its central characteristic, a love that will risk itself for one's friend. Love is linked once more to obedience in verse 14. Jesus called his disciples "friends," not servants, and introduced them to an intimate fellowship with his Father similar to his own. From this point on the disciples (i.e., the Church) enter into a new relationship with Christ—*friends* of Christ.

The initiative is always with God. The disciples, like Jesus, were to be fruit bearers (see Gal. 5:22, 23), to enter into a new prayer relation with God and, supremely, to love one another.

Reflection: Verses 1–5. Where is your place of abiding? Where is your security? What is your point of reference for decision making? I often go to bed so conscious of work undone and of the amount of work to be done tomorrow. Too often achievement is my security. I take refuge in doing rather than in being.

List some of the ways that God "prunes" (disciplines) us. Sickness? Reversals? Persecution (see vv. 18–20)? Permitting temptation? What has been the result of God's "pruning"? Note three phases of abiding: "In me" (v. 4); "My words in you" (v. 7); "In my love" (v. 9). Is your life fruitful? Check this through with Galatians 5:22, 23.

Verses 9–17. The theme moves from abiding and fruit-bearing to the flow of love. Read verses 9 and 12 in sequence. God's love, the kind that we see in Jesus, comes through the indwelling Christ into our lives, and we live it out in our daily relationships with others.

I find I am overwhelmed by this dimension of love. I am unable fully to love this way. I find I want to settle for kindness, consideration, or doing my share of the work. But a love that lays down its life regardless of what the other fellow does! No way! For example, I take my wife shopping and park the car where I can see the exit so as not to keep her waiting and proceed to read the book I have brought along. She has said she will be 45 minutes. I read leisurely, glad of the opportunity. But suddenly, I look at my watch. She's been gone an hour! Why is she late? What's the matter? I have enough love (or should I say kindness) for 45 minutes, but not for an hour! The twelve-year-old does not come home from school at 3:30 when expected. To be in by 4:00 or 4:30 would have been all right, but he comes at 6:30 with a beatific smile on his face. Worried, you may have phoned the school, the neighbors. Now you pounce on him without even waiting to hear his story. How easily our love runs short when plans we have made go awry. We are ready to love on our terms, if people fit into our expectations!

Sacrificial love is quite another matter. Such love goes on loving others when they shirk, disappoint, wound or even betray. This was the love of Jesus, and this is what his love will do through us as we abide in him.

Living in a Hostile World

Read John 15:18–16:4a

Comment: The disciples were to expect to receive the same kind of treatment from the world as had their Master. The world's hatred would be one evidence that the disciples were Jesus' chosen people. If the world truly knew God, it would love Jesus and his disciples (i.e., the Church). But the world, like the religious leaders (see 8:23), is "from below" and Jesus is "from above"; therefore the world will hate them.

Verses 26, 27. God will send them a Counselor (variously translated, Comforter, Helper, Advocate) to be with them through their trials and persecution. He will witness to the power and truth of Jesus so that the disciples may not falter in their witness.

Verses 1–4a. John returns to the subject of the world's hatred. These words are spoken so that in the trauma of persecution they will be able to remain steadfast as they recall what their Master said and did.

Reflection: Verses 18–21. Men mete out hostility both to those who choose evil pathways and to those who choose the good. We cannot escape it. But to be hated because we are his chosen people is to be reminded that we walk in Jesus' footsteps, and thus opportunity is given us to be his witnesses (v. 27). I must confess that I stir up very little hatred. I want so much to be liked! This causes me to ask myself, *In what ways am I failing my Master?*

Verses 22–24. The presence of Christ can bring blessing or curse. I find that the more I learn about Jesus the greater the moral demands that are laid on me. The more I grow in Christ the greater is my sense of responsibility toward others. To turn my back on Christ at this point is not only sin but will end in my hating the Christ I disobey. But when I joyously respond to Christ's call I am blessed and fulfilled.

When you encounter hostility what is your response? Evil for evil? Withdrawal? Stubbornness? Or the witness of a victorious, forgiving love?

Note that the literal meaning of *witness* is "martyr"—one who lays down his life for what he believes. How often I have witnessed bravely with words that have exceeded my lifestyle, and I have preached beyond the level of my experience! Is our witness largely word and profession or one of steadfast, sacrificial, forgiving love?

Verses 26–4a. When has the Counselor, the Holy Spirit, borne witness of Jesus in your life? When has he helped you to remember what Jesus has told you? Think of the perspective of memory: verses learned in childhood come to mind in times of crisis; promises that you have proved true are recalled in another time of critical decision; the assurance of Jesus' presence wells up through your soul when you stand alone against people or circumstances. Recall some of these occasions of remembering in your life.

The Advantage of the Invisible
Read John 16:4b–15

Comment: These verses, 16:4b–15, comprise the last two sections on the Holy Spirit (see *Comment* on 14:16, 17).

Verses 4b–11. As long as Jesus is bodily present they will lean on him. When the Counselor comes he will be an invisible Presence within them. The Greek word for Counselor is *Paraclete;* literally, one who is called alongside. The disciples are thus enabled to live without the physical presence of Jesus. They will grow strong as they respond to the wisdom and inner leading of the Counselor. This would be to their advantage (v. 7).

Verses 8–11. We now see the Counselor as Advocate, as one who will convince the world in three areas:

With respect to sin: Jesus revealed that the trust in law and tradition by the religious leaders had failed, and the Greeks' trust in reason and knowledge had fallen short. Man's sinfulness stands exposed and powerless.

With respect to righteousness: The resurrection and ascension (Jesus' going to the Father) have reversed the seeming victory of the world at Calvary and proven Jesus to be the Victor, the Righteous One.

With respect to judgment: The Counselor will also reverse the judgment of Calvary. Jesus, not Pilate, was right. Pilate and the world are the ones who stand under judgment. Sin has overreached itself and stands condemned. While these three pronouncements will come true at the Last Day, they are made true for us in the contemporary scene by the presence of the Counselor in our lives now.

The Spirit would both interpret what they had heard and would continue and complete Jesus' teaching for his disciples. The Spirit will glorify Jesus, that is, he will show Jesus to be the Messiah, the Logos of God, the One truly sent of God.

Reflection: Let me summarize *my personal pilgrimage* in regard to the Spirit. I read the Gospels to discover the lifestyle and spirit of the historical Jesus. I believe in this Jesus; that he is the Son of God, the Messiah, the one sent from his Father to reveal God to me. As I read I am impressed; I admire; I worship; I give myself to him and his Kingdom. I love him for his life and for his death on Calvary. I dedicate my all to him and resolve to follow him, and to be an obedient disciple.

The Jesus of history has entered my life as the risen Christ of experience. He also sends the Counselor, the Spirit of truth, to be with me forever. The risen Christ and the Spirit are within me as united evidence of the presence of the indwelling God. The words of the Gospel come alive for me as the Spirit prompts me: urging, restraining, instructing, bringing to mind Jesus' teachings. The more I listen, am aware, and obey, the more I will hear the Spirit and respond to his guidance.

What is the Gospel saying to you? Who is this Jesus we are reading about and what does he mean to you? Could you journal, briefly or at length, the story of *your personal pilgrimage?*

Brief Sorrow—Lasting Joy
Read John 16:16–24

Comment: The sorrow occasioned by Jesus' death was to be turned into joy. The departure was only for a little while. He would return! A woman's pain in childbirth is forgotten when her child is born. As the new age is born the disciples will forget their sorrow and rejoice with unending joy (v. 22).

Jesus was saying, "When I return your joy will be so complete that you will want nothing more, and ask nothing. If however you do ask, God will answer your request according to my wishes and plans for you. Practice asking according to my will and God will give to you in abundance and with joy."

Reflection: This brings us once again to the death-resurrection motif. Are we willing to suffer gladly now in order to gain long-term reward, or do we live for the quick gain and seek present comfort? Do we feel we have earned the right to retire from life's responsibilities and let someone else shoulder the load? A Christian is called to unending responsibility and an unending ministry of love and reconciliation because he has resident in him the eternal, caring love and grace of God. But this God is also calling us to unending victory and joy. Every once in a while I find myself saying, "I've gone as far as I'm going to and now it's the other fellow's turn." There may be a barrier between myself and my wife. Stubbornly I am waiting for her to be the first to apologize. Or it may be that I am a little tense or uptight and I refuse to take time to let God tell me where I am at fault and to let him center me down in himself. I just go on working and pressuring to get things done.

Verses 22–24. In what ways are you experiencing the return of Jesus? The daily indwelling of the Spirit? The joy of answered prayer?

On the days that I feel Jesus Christ flooding into my heart, I find I want nothing else. My joy is full. I only desire more of this same wonderful Christ!

The Cry of Victory

Read John 16:25–33

Comment: Verses 25–27. It is difficult to describe a landscape or clouds or the ocean to someone who is blind. One must speak in analogies and figures of speech. So also it was difficult to tell the disciples about God. Because of their legalistic nature they had boxed God in as austere, wrathful and distant—a stern Judge. Finally their eyes were opening. It is as though they were saying, "Is God really like you,

Master?" and as if Jesus replied, "Yes, he is. If you have seen me you have really seen the Father, and what is most important is that not only I but my Father himself loves you."

Verse 28. "In four short phrases we have the Pre-existence of Christ (came from the Father); His Incarnation (have come into the world); His death (leaving the world) and His ascension (going to the Father)" (Wilbert F. Howard, "Introduction and Exegesis to the Gospel According to St. John," *The Interpreter's Bible,* 8:739).

Verses 29–32. The response of the disciples was a warm confession of faith (cp. Mark 8:29). They believed that Jesus had indeed come from God, that he was who he said he was. Jesus warns them of how soon they will desert him. But they are to be of "good cheer" because he is winning the victory for them. Their hope and peace is not to be found within themselves, but in their Master.

Reflection: What childhood memories are awakened as you think of God? As a child I wondered why tragic things happened. I recall the death of a schoolmate from tuberculosis. I can still hear his hacking cough. I remember a picture in the family Bible showing the earth opening up and people falling headlong into the chasm. I wondered why God let my parents be separated. I blamed God for these things and much else. I believed that Jesus was loving, but I was afraid of God. What were your childhood experiences of God? Have you worked through such memories? Can you accept at face value, with the open-heartedness of a little child, that God is your Father and loves you on his own initiative?

Where is the ground of your hope, the source of your peace? Is it in your ability to overcome or in the victory that Christ has already won for you? How can you transfer the basis of your confidence and good cheer from yourself to Jesus Christ? As we daily transfer the ground of our faith from ourselves to Christ (by dying to ourselves with him that we may rise with him), then also daily we can be overcomers and share in his cry of victory: "Be of good cheer, I have overcome the world."

VIII

The High Priestly Prayer
(John 17:1–26)

Jesus' Prayer for Himself

Read John 17:1–5

Comment: This chapter, often called the High Priestly Prayer, brings to a close the discourse which began in 13:31. It was characteristic of Jewish discourses to close with prayer which often, as here, was the climax of all that had been said before. The prayer divides itself naturally into three sections:

Jesus' prayer for himself (1–5); for his disciples (6–19); for the universal Church (20–26).

Verses 1–5. The hour of death now has come, but Jesus speaks of it as glorification. By his life and death he has revealed the Father. Slowly the disciples have come to know God through him and are entering into eternal life.

Two things were uppermost in Jesus' mind: that he would honor his Father and that he might bring eternal life to those who believe. But to do this he must himself be glorified, that is, be crucified and rise again. Only in this way will men know he came from and returns to God. In verses 3 and 4 he claims by faith the power to go to the cross and accomplish the work. He speaks of it as having already taken place and believes God will glorify him by returning him to the place of honor he held before he came to earth. In today's language, Jesus is the middleman (the Mediator) between two interested parties, God and man.

Reflection: John omits Jesus' struggle in Gethsemane. The High Priestly Prayer psychologically follows his anguish in the garden. It is the victorious prayer of someone who is no longer wrestling with temptation, but is now by faith standing in a triumphant stance.

We need both kinds of prayers: to wrestle for victory and to walk confidently by faith. What is your customary manner of praying? Are you in the main a *struggling* or a *victorious* pilgrim? There will be times of struggle (as with Jesus in Gethsemane) when we grow in Christ by facing the issues in life. But our accustomed lifestyle can be one of confident and triumphant faith as exemplified in Jesus.

Jesus' Prayer for His Disciples
Read John 17:6–19

Comment: In this prayer for his disciples Jesus asks no material comfort, no special treatment! They, like their Master, must live in a hostile world. Jesus' prayer claims the future as now present. He sees his disciples through the eyes of faith as having already become the persons he believed they would become. Now they know that it is God who sent Jesus and who has been speaking and working through him.

Verses 7–17. He prays for them for three reasons: because they are God's gift to him; because he has been glorified in them; because they will be left without Jesus' presence in the flesh. He prays (a) that despite his leaving them, they will live in the same quality of unity that he himself experiences with God (v. 11); (b) that they will be filled with his joy in spite of the world's hatred (v. 13); (c) that although remaining in the world they will be kept from evil (v. 15); and finally (d) that they may be sanctified in the truth (v. 17). The word *sanctify* denotes separation from the sin of the world plus dedication and equipment for God's service.

Reflection: What can we learn from Jesus' way of praying? Verses 6 through 8 represent Jesus as reviewing what had taken place between himself and his disciples. They were God's gift to him; he had taught them as God willed; now he declared what was not immediately true, namely that they believed that Jesus was sent by God. This was an act of faith on Jesus' part, later to be realized.

I frequently find when I sit down for my devotions that the first thing I must do is briefly review what has happened recently and locate where I am in spirit. Am I hurried? Worried? Am I rejoicing in the day or threatened by it? How do I feel in my heart in relation to my family and associates? I must first become aware of the self in me that I am offering to God that morning.

Verses 9–19. Jesus prays that his disciples will stay in the world, yet not be of it, even as he was not of the world.

I am troubled that I live in a little village away from the corrosive problems of the world: ghettos, poverty, corruption, pollution. In one sense I am not truly living in today's world. And even here, I find a tendency to withdraw from the world in which I do live: to avoid encounter with family or friends, to live in a world of fantasy rather than reality. What is your experience? To what extent are you involved or refusing to be involved?

Verse 19. I remember the first time this verse came alive for me. I was dating my wife-to-be while in college. It was a case of love at first sight. Every afternoon we took our books and walked hand in hand along the bank of the nearby river to find a quiet spot to study and talk. We were both strong Christians. We started each afternoon's fellowship with Bible reading and prayer. But I was a lonely boy— one parent dead, the other far away in England. I longed for love and affection. The battle to keep my love disciplined was becoming increasingly difficult. I was torn—the sex impulses were saying "yes, yes"; my past training and the church were saying, "no, no."

I had read this High Priestly Prayer out loud as we sat together. In the silence I went back to the nineteenth verse. Its meaning was apparent: Jesus' dedication of himself to the highest was for the sake of his disciples, so that he could be a worthy leader for them.

Suddenly the words leaped out of the page for me. I, who was in conflict over my desire to be more intimate, was fighting the battle in terms of duty, ethics, fear and a host of other pressures from without. But it should be an inner urging, "for their sakes." As I sat there I thought that maybe this was the girl I would marry (at least, I hoped so) and then there would be children. *For their sakes,* for these children yet unborn, I'll fight my battle. There was a shift in the scene of battle. Not an outward keeping of rules but an inner surge of purpose. I felt a rush of joy together with a new discipline of love. In the course of time we were married, and in the wedding ring the words are engraved: "For their sakes—John 17:19." I received abundant reward for the battle when I held our firstborn in my arms—and even deeper joy when I said to our teenagers one by one as they began to date: "Most parents give advice and tell their children what not to do. Instead of that, I'd like to tell you a story of a battle your mother and I fought and won for you."

Jesus' Prayer for the Church

Read John 17:20–26

Comment: Verses 20–23. The main thrust of this section of the prayer is for unity—that those who believe in him (the coming Church) may be *one.* The basis of this unity is to be that which exists between God and Jesus. When this takes place the world will know that Jesus is the Sent One, the Messiah of God. The glory of Jesus is to be the Church's glory. But this is a death-resurrection glory. One can only enter into this glory as he follows the path of self-denial in every situation as did Jesus. Verses 22 and 23 contain the hope that all who believe may share in his eternal glory both on earth and forever. The closing prayer of Jesus is that all who believe in him will be with him in his glory and will be the recipients of the same love which God has given to him.

Reflection: Christians everywhere are included in this prayer, for we ourselves believe in Christ through the disciples' word (v. 20). Every thought and sentence of this prayer can be personally appropriated as spoken directly to each of us. The emphasis on unity speaks strongly to any of us who refuse to share communion with fellow Christians, to those newly quickened converts who so easily break away from churches, to those who would be divisive, spreading distrust and hostility between church groups.

How do you define unity? Is it agreement? Docile acceptance? Common purpose? Avoidance or acceptance of encounter? Thinking alike? Voting the same way? Consensus? Is there a dynamic, painful process at work in achieving unity? What produces unity? Jesus said, "I and my Father are one." Yet this oneness was wrought by agonizing wrestling in Gethsemane. He had a sense of mission (sentness), of obedience to his Father. With joy he laid down his life for others. Could a group of which you are a part (family, friends, church) find a basis of unity through these steps? How would you go about it?

Unity is more difficult in the higher echelons of life: between parents themselves rather than between parents and children, between the leaders of a business than among the rank and file, or between the clergy of a multiministry staff in a church. It was the reverse in Jesus' case. The top echelon for him was God and he, and *they were One.* What evidences of growth toward unity do you see taking place where you have responsibility? Consider the destructive effect of power play, jealousy, fear. Consider on the other hand the value of the Christ-qualities of openness, the death-resurrection motif.

Verse 26. We are heirs to the very love with which God loved Jesus (see again 14:23). It is authenticated by the presence of the Spirit of the risen Christ who dwells in us forever.

IX

Gethsemane to Calvary
(John 18:1–19:42)

Kingly Strength

Read John 18:1–11

Comment: In the foregoing discourses (chaps. 14–17) John has interrupted his narrative of the Passion in order to relate something of the teaching and philosophy of Jesus. These discourses have been concluded and the writer returns to the narrative which we left in 13:30, at the point when Judas went out into the night to complete the arrangements for the betrayal. Judas now returns to the garden and the Gospel story concludes with the arrest, trial, crucifixion, burial, discovery of the empty tomb and the appearance of the risen Christ to his disciples (chaps. 18–21).

The night setting of the betrayal is significant. Jesus is the Light of the world, but Judas dwells in darkness. So, too, do the soldiers and police. In their night they must bring lanterns and torches.

Verses 4–8. The simplicity of Jesus' speech to those coming to take him reveals his dignity and authority. It is not the world but the Christ who rules the situation. Recall the words, "I lay [my life] down of my own accord" (10:18).

In contrast Peter imitates the world by resorting to violent action.

Verse 11. The glorification Jesus has spoken of earlier can only take place if he is obedient to his Father's will and lays down his life in sacrificial death.

Reflection: Unfaithfulness and betrayal often take place at night, under cover, in secret. One test of an act being wrong for me is if I do it secretly and do not wish others to know of it. Do you experience this?

The garden was a place made sacred by Jesus' frequent visits and his talks with the disciples. Judas profaned the sacred. What are ways that we profane the holy? Do we use the church for social climbing or the advancement of our points of view? Do we use Bible verses for our own ego trips? Our children for our own gratification? Other persons as things to satisfy our ego or our lust?

Note the irreversible quality of sin. No doubt Judas in his remorse would have liked to undo what he had done—both for Jesus' sake and his own—but it was too late. Can you think of a time when you have grievously hurt another or yourself by some sin? Some careless word? Some bit of unkind gossip? It cannot be undone, but it can be forgiven by the grace of God.

Peter sought to aid Jesus by the wrong means—the sword to rescue the Prince of Peace! He used the weapons of the enemy. When a friend of yours has been wrongly judged or bitterly attacked, do you return evil for evil? With what weapons of love can you support your friend?

Four Kinds of Response

Read John 18:12–27

Comment: In this section the story of Jesus' questioning before Annas (vv. 19–24) is framed by the two accounts of Peter's denial (vv. 15–18 and 25–27). Jesus and Peter are portrayed in marked contrast to each other: "Jesus stands up to his questioners and denies nothing, while Peter cowers before his questioners and denies everything" (Brown, *The Gospel According to John; The Anchor Bible,* vol. 29A, p. 842).

Peter is warming himself in verse 18. When we return to the Peter narrative in verse 25 he is still standing by that same fire! During all of this time, Jesus stood unafraid, speaking out boldly to Annas and later to the man who struck him. This section ends with Peter's third denial and the cock crowing.

Reflection: Consider these people in turn:

Peter: shivering, afraid, immobilized, cornered into denial.

Annas: insensitive, callous, unknowing, proud of his position of power.

The soldiers: brutal, "all in a day's work," violent in frustration.

Jesus: speaking forthrightly, acting with authority and courage, standing in two worlds.

I find something of all four of them in me! Like Peter I can fail to declare myself as a follower of Christ when the time is ripe for such a declaration in everyday contacts. Like Annas there are times when I am very insensitive to the needs or loneliness of another. I would not dream of *acting* with brutality as did the soldiers, but I have fantasized myself as doing very unkind things to get even with someone. Yes, and there are times when I have spoken forthrightly and acted with courage as did Jesus, finding strength from the unseen world. What a strange mixture I am! What is your response to these four lifestyles?

In the last section (18:1–11) Judas betrayed Jesus. In this section we read of Peter's denial of Jesus. Let us contrast the two: In the struggle between good and evil, light and darkness, Judas chose the evil and darkness. He betrayed the Christ. Matthew's Gospel says that he "repented . . . saying 'I have sinned . . .' and he went and hanged himself" (Matt. 27:3–5).

Peter chose differently. He had previously declared himself a disciple and affirmed his loyalty to Jesus. But he was humanly fallible. He resorted to force in the garden. In the alien territory of the Judeans, he was afraid and denied his Lord. But he wept, repented and began again. He was emerging into the Light. He could be, and was, used mightly by Christ.

What Is Truth?

Read John 18:28–40

Comment: John treats Jesus' trial before Pilate at much greater length than the one before the Jewish authorities.

As with Annas, so now before Pilate: Jesus spoke forthrightly and bore witness to his Kingship in a manner that ultimately led to his death. Pilate was relieved to know Jesus was not a political king, but mystified by Jesus' claim to be a spiritual King whose mission was to reveal the truth.

Jesus stood before Pilate as a King. Kingship carried with it the authority to judge. What irony that the roles are reversed! Pilate, who legally had power to judge Jesus, found himself judged. History has reversed the verdict Pilate rendered. Jesus as the Christ is the world's Judge. The penetrating light of his life uncovers evil and people stand self-condemned.

Jesus stood there as Truth (14:6). He was truth in the sense that he was from God and one with him and therefore one with reality, *truly real*. He was truth in that to know him is to live in the freedom of an abundant life. Pilate represented force, repression and political opportunism. Jesus set people free to be children of God and heirs of eternal life.

Reflection: These Jewish leaders were willing to kill from envy and hate but refused to enter the Gentile Praetorium lest they be defiled!

Church people can sometimes do dastardly things and yet be quite meticulous about keeping church traditions. Someone who is always on time to teach a Sunday school class can ruin a person's life through gossip. Deacons who serve the elements at Communion can vote against admitting Christians who are members of minority groups into the church. All of us in varying degrees separate our faith from our actions.

What inconsistencies do you see in your life?

Jesus recognized that Pilate could not grasp either the spiritual significance of his Kingship or that he, Jesus, stood there as the embodiment of Truth. Pilate's training had conditioned him to think of a king only in political terms and he could not comprehend one who was enthroned King of people's lives. Does your early training make it more difficult for you to see spiritual values? Do you legalistically see all persons who are found legally guilty as always morally guilty? Can nations and citizens be so convinced that weapons and missiles are the only way to be secure in relation to other nations that they discount or even ignore the power and methods of love? Jesus as Truth was free—free to love and obey God, free to be himself and to be one with his Father, free to love all varieties of humankind. He was free to live or to die.

Pilate was not free. He wanted to be decent and fair. But he must not upset the applecart. He must keep the peace at any price, even if it meant ordering the death of an innocent man.

The religious leaders were not free. They were bound to their traditions and ideology. Legalism took precedence over love.

The indwelling Christ comes to set each of us free today: free to love God and be heir to his Spirit; free to be ourselves with an ever-growing I AM within each of us, free to love our fellowman at whatever cost.

Jesus is the Truth and as he lives in us we are free and victorious against the temporal powers of state and the fanatical and ideological pressures of modern society.

Jesus and Pilate

Read John 19:1–16

Comment: Pilate, convinced of Jesus' innocence, had failed to gain his release by offering Barabbas to the mob. He then tried to assuage their blood lust by having Jesus scourged and humiliated. Jesus must have presented a pitiable sight, exhausted and in agony from the scourging, covered with blood from the thorns. The words "Behold the man" could well have meant, "You don't mean to tell me that you are afraid of this weak and pitiful figure. Why not let him go? What harm can he do?" In John's mind, Jesus was indeed *Man,* the word made flesh. But he was also *King* (come from above). This was the Messiah, the Suffering Servant, who was laying down his life knowing that the path to resurrection and eternal life lay through self-giving, even through death itself.

The priest-driven mob cried out more vehemently, "Crucify him!" (v. 6). When Pilate delayed further, they blurted out the real reason for their hatred: "He has made himself the Son of God." Here is religious fanaticism at its worst.

Pilate was disturbed and questioned Jesus again. Beneath Jesus' silence was the regal authority of one who knew who he was and what he had to do. Jesus stated that *all* power was given of God, given of course to be used with justice and mercy. By falsely accusing Jesus before Pilate, the Jewish leaders were grossly misusing their power.

Pilate's resistance was finally broken when the mob played up Jesus' Kingship against that of Caesar. Pilate, seeing his position threatened, reluctantly capitulated with, "Here is your King." What depths of fanaticism the mob revealed as the shout rang out, "We have no king but Caesar," a statement that none of them believed in their saner moments! What irony that he whom they sneeringly called king was indeed King and would live on to overthrow mighty Rome!

Reflection: In "Christ and Pilate" artist Max Beckmann presents Pilate facing a Christ-figure who is totally without form or comeliness. Lionel Whiston, Jr., comments, "Weak, ugly, bleeding, drab: is this the one who should prevail? Opposite Jesus is Pilate. Sure of himself, patronizing, entrenched in power—can there be any doubt where the wave of the future rests? Yet you and I know that one of the figures is the great liberating hero and that the other's name is synonymous with weakness. Here is an inversion of values: the latent power of weakness, the corrosive weakness of power. Easter proclaims the deceptiveness of appearance and announces the coronation of right. So I take my stance in the 'now' of this present moment with its grotesque distortion of values. In so doing I know with Beckman where is the victory."

Where are the false and where are the real values in the nation, the church, your life?

In the nation, what is our right to excessive gasoline consumption, thereby diminishing supplies for our children's children? Consider the ethics of waste in excessive packaging and nonreturnable containers versus stewardship of

God's material gifts. Think of other situations similar to these.

In the church, do we overvalue the high rating of numbers and a pledged budget as compared with the degree of loving concern among members of the congregation? Do we value the desire to have the right people in church above the love of Jesus who associated with the hated Roman sympathizers and prostitutes? Do we value money, social status and success over the more ultimate values of caring love, sacrificial service and ministry to the underprivileged?

In your life, to what extent do you stand up for the principles you know to be right when pressures come from neighbors, friends, society? What about abandoning parental standards as other parents do? Failing to report pollution, inadequate safety standards, inferior products because of the danger of losing your job? Forsaking Christian ideals of love and caring toward someone when your peers or community have adopted an attitude of hostility toward that person? Withdrawing from problems by flight from the city, retreat from encounters with minority groups, the resort to quick, easy money or ample pensions that provide unlimited leisure? The Spirit of Jesus would seem to direct us toward encounter, costly involvement, creativity and the service of our fellows as long as we live. Evaluate your attitudes and behavior.

The Ultimate Sacrifice

Read John 19:17–30

Comment: What irony that the inscription over the cross intended as a jeer to both Jesus and the Jews proved to be prophetic of the universal Lordship of Christ. It was trilingual: the Latin reminds us that Jesus is to be enthroned in the political world, King of kings; the Greek suggests that culture and civilization find their lasting values in him; the Hebrew unwittingly affirms Jesus to be the fulfillment of true religion. He is Lord of all of life.

Verses 26–30. There are three utterances from the Cross in this Gospel: The first revealed Jesus' self-forgetfulness despite his personal agony. He thought of and provided for his mother. The second, "I thirst," was not play acting. It was a human cry from an exhausted, dehydrated body. The last one was the final victory shout, "It is finished."

Reflection: Jesus modeled what he taught. The heart of his message was that the pathway to resurrection lay through death. Jesus freely accepted death, even called it being glorified! (12:23). Suffering and death are thrust on the secular man. But the Christian embraces them. Comment on how well you model what you believe and how well you accept suffering and death. What do the three languages of the inscription on the Cross say to you?

Political: If your party's candidate's position conflicts with the Spirit of Christ which way do you vote? What decides your political viewpoint? The media? Your peers? The Sermon on the Mount?

Cultural: To what extent are the TV and newspapers affecting your thinking and your ideals? Are you giving up reading the great classics for easier TV? By-passing the great music of the centuries for the fleeting tunes of the day? Is Christ "King" in your tastes and cultural choices?

Religious: Is the Spirit of Christ at the heart of your churchmanship? Which is primary, maintaining an institution or building relationships with God and persons? In a word, is Christ the Lord of your total life?

Consider the three sayings from the cross:

In the agony of dying, Jesus thought of two lonely people— his mother and a young friend. I find that the mildest sickness can sometimes throw me into a state of self-reference and self-concern. How is it with you?

The words "I thirst" show Jesus to be a man of like feelings with us. Can you relate more easily to Christ when you know this? What does his weariness of body, his agony of soul say to you? How does he become a closer Companion?

The final words "It is finished" reveal Jesus as One who lived a life of fulfillment. He was able to say, "It is finished" at his death because he could say it after each task, after each day's work. Do you go to bed each night fulfilled or unfulfilled? How can you receive this sense of daily fulfillment? Are you looking forward to your final victory shout, "Thank you, God, it is finished"?

That You May Believe

Read John 19:31–37

Comment: Verse 31. It was contrary to Jewish law for a body to hang on a tree overnight (see Deut. 21:22–23). The breaking of the legs hastened death. The Jews wanted to be sure he was dead and that they were rid of him.

Verses 34–35. The appearance of blood and water is underscored by John in verse 35. That we may believe, he wants us to know it really happened and it had a deeper meaning. Note the similarity to 20:31. Blood and water suggest the Sacraments, the Communion and Baptism. We recall the words, "my blood is drink indeed" (6:55), and "out of his heart shall flow rivers of living water" (7:38). We are cleansed and forgiven as by faith the Living Water of Baptism touches our lives. We receive divine transfusion from above as by faith we drink his "blood"—the New Wine of the Living Vine—receiving into our lives the risen Christ and with him eternal life.

Reflection: What an obscenity when, in the name of religion, men trump up false charges out of envy and cause the torturous killing of an innocent man, and then further call on their religious rules to painfully hasten death so the bodies could be removed and the Sabbath not profaned! Are there blind spots in your religious practices? Are white collar crimes less evil to you than crimes on the street? Are you less likely to perceive wrong in a strong church worker than in one who never attends church? In what ways do we sanction behavior that is contrary to the Spirit of Jesus?

John was seeking to tell us that the death of Jesus was part of a death-resurrection event. Jesus had come from God, lived in flesh as a human being, offered up his life of his own free will, stood firm in his witness before his judges, been faithful to the death. Through his death he returns risen and victorious to God, sending the Holy Spirit and to live within us as the risen Christ.

To read of the crucifixion can be merely to read a sad and humiliating story or it can, by a leap of faith, be an act of participation whereby the living water and the life-giving blood of Christ flow into our lives.

What happens when you receive the bread and the cup at the Communion Service? Nothing, just a pleasant custom? A nice warm glow? A temporary lift? The words "blood and water" (v. 34) are intended to convey the truth that, as we call to mind the crucified Christ, we can by faith receive Christ into our lives as the living Water that forever cleanses and refreshes us. We can receive the blood, the spiritual plasma, of Christ empowering us and imparting to us a quality of life that is forever. John says that he recounts this story of the crucifixion that we may believe, (v. 35), i.e., have faith, a faith that lays hold of the terrific truth that the risen Christ, the living Water and the life-giving Blood, is ours daily and forever. Personally, this staggers my imagination. Yet each time I receive the elements at Communion I seek with childlike faith to believe this. What is your experience?

Disciples Take a Stand

Read John 19:38–42

Comment: Joseph and Nicodemus were men of standing, VIPs. Nicodemus brought a very generous, even extraordinary, supply of spices and oils for an elaborate burial. At the time when the twelve had deserted and it seemed that this Jesus hanging on a cross was completely discredited, these two men took their stand. They abandoned their past secrecy and risked disfavor and even ostracism from their fellow members of the Sanhedrin. An act of sterling courage!

Reflection: Was the excessive amount of spices, like Mary Magdalene's reckless use of ointment, an unconscious expression of guilt revealing that Nicodemus wished he had believed more deeply in this Rabbi while he was alive? Where do you find yourself overcompensating? What does this say about your inability to receive God's forgiveness or to forgive yourself?

Are you in some respects a "secret disciple"? Do you speak out and take a stand for what you believe as often as you should? What holds you back? Does the recollection of Jesus' death on the cross give you courage to be more open and loyal to Christ? What forms could this new loyalty take?

X

Appearances of the Risen Lord
(John 20:1–29)

Graveclothes to Living Garments

Read John 20:1–10

Comment: Verse 1. Other women may have been with Mary Magdalene. See "we" in verse 2. For further comment on Mary Magdalene, see 20:11–18.

Verse 2. The empty tomb cannot be rationally explained. For me the most satisfactory comment is one by Dr. C. F. D. Moule (quoted by Brown in *The Gospel According to John; The Anchor Bible,* vol. 29A, p. 978): "The idea that Jesus' body is no longer in the tomb is not just an interesting detail about his victory over death but is essential to understanding a major aspect in Christian theology, namely that what God creates is not destroyed, but is re-created and transformed."

Verse 3. The "other disciple" is often regarded as being John himself, a considerably younger man than Peter, hence arriving first.

Verse 8. Again the purpose of the Gospel! John *believed* (see v. 31).

Reflection: Verses 3–9. The impetuous Peter rushed in and

John, hesitant and awe-struck, finally followed after. Peter, in spite of his brash entry, could not understand what had happened. John contemplatively remembered what Jesus had said and believed.

Note the difference in the two temperaments, yet how God used both. Peter boldly rushed in, saw but did not understand; later John, hesitant, afraid, followed the leader but discovered some things hidden from the bolder man. Toward which of these temperaments do you lean? Think through the ways in which God uses the "you" that you are. Comment on the unconscious influence that Peter's bold act had on John. Consider the unconscious influence of your life on others.

The graveclothes were left behind. Living persons do not wear the garments of death. Are there any remnants of death in you which if kept will kill out the good (the God)? What are some of the garments of death that you have worn? What are the garments of your new life in Christ?

Are significant events taking place in your generation without your comprehending what is really happening? How few people sensed the meaning of the resurrection event at the time! Where is God breaking through with newness of life today? The emphasis on openness and honesty? The recognition of the work of the Holy Spirit? The revolt of suppressed nations and minority groups? The prolific sale of religious literature? Is God trying to say something to us? If so, what?

He Is Alive!

Read John 20:11-18

Comment: Jesus said that one who is forgiven little loves little, but the one forgiven much loves much (Luke 7:47). John places Mary Magdalene, a forgiven, redeemed prostitute, as the first at the tomb and the first to see the risen Lord. Her heart is breaking that this Man who has shown and taught her a new way of living and loving has been killed. She had watched the cruelty of the crucifixion. The hours had dragged wearily until early Sunday. Before dawn she was there! She was seeking this Man who had opened to her the door to new hope.

In the darkness she did not recognize Jesus. But when he called her by name as he often had before, she immediately responded, "Rabboni," that is, "My dearest Teacher." As she started to embrace him, Jesus said, "You must not cling to me" (Goodspeed). Jesus' warm embrace in the past had mediated God's love to her, made her feel not the object of a man's lust, but a child of God, a woman of infinite worth.

But to embrace him now would have been to hold on to the earthly Jesus. Mary had not yet realized that the Jesus she knew was to become a spiritual Presence, the indwelling Christ. She must let go her hold on the human, earthly Jesus and see him as ascended and returning to live as the risen Christ within her. Then she would know that his Father was her Father, his God was her God. God and Christ would come to make their home in her (14:23). This was the message she was to give to the disciples—that he lived and would be with them forever.

Reflection: Mary Magdalene was forgiven much. The greater the sin, the greater the grace. Is *sin* becoming too old-fashioned a word for us? Do we tend to call our sins by other names: improprieties, mistakes, illegalities, lapses of conscience? There can only be an outpouring of God's grace when we come as repentant sinners. No sin, no grace! Try as I may to avoid seeing myself as a sinner, I am impelled again and again to return to God with the words,

"God, forgive me. I have sinned." It is then that I experience his grace and know his love. Think through your experience: Was there a gradual or a sudden conversion? Was there repentance, forgiveness and the inflow of God's grace? Is this a continuing process? Are there "cement walls" that you've said you'll never tear down, places where you'll never change?

What is this encounter between Jesus and Mary saying to you?

The warm embrace and kiss between the sexes can be the occasion of God's affirming love to one another in a beautiful way. The frequency of touch in Jesus' life suggests he knew and used body language and used the embrace in this way. We have every reason to believe that Jesus expressed God's love freely to men and women alike. Yet it is consonant with Jesus' life and teaching to believe that he kept his love relationships under discipline. Paul starts the list of fruits of the Spirit with "love" but ends it with "self-control" (Gal. 5:22). The same Spirit who releases love in and through us will warn us when that love is becoming possessive, directive, self-centered or lustful and will help us to keep it under his discipline and control.

Are you free to express love to God's other children? Are you comfortable affirming your love to both men and women? Should you be more free? If you do feel free to express love to the same or the opposite sex is there need for more discipline and self-control? Is the physical embrace ever a substitute for costly spiritual encounter? On the other hand, we often continue talking and arguing when instead there should be a kiss or an embrace. What is God's word to you about this?

When Mary heard Jesus speak her name, she was transfixed with wonder. I frequently write letters to God. Then after a reflective pause I write what I believe to be God's answer to me. As I begin the reply "Dear Lee" and end it, "Your Heavenly Father," I feel an awe and yet a closeness. My God is calling me by name! As I ponder his words of affirmation and love, I feel like crying aloud with Mary, "I have seen the Lord" (v. 18)!

Verse 17. Jesus' ascent into heaven freed him from bodily limitations and makes him available now to all of us as the risen Christ. This is the Good News for us to proclaim.

The Risen Christ Returns
Read John 20:19–29

Comment: Verses 19–22. The mention of shut doors was to emphasize the spiritual nature of the risen Christ as opposed to the human quality of Jesus' body before the resurrection. "Peace be with you" *(shalom)* was a customary Jewish greeting. Peace is what Jesus came to bring and by his death and resurrection has now brought. The risen Christ said to his disciples, "As the Father has sent me, even so I send you." In other words, "I have done it; now I am asking you to do the same." The disciples (pupils) were now to become apostles (commissioned and sent). And immediately he adds, "Receive the Holy Spirit," for the Spirit of Christ could only be given after his resurrection. Thus they are sent out in the Spirit's power and not in their own strength. From now on he is to be with them.

Verse 23. Jesus had the power to forgive sins and now with the coming of the Holy Spirit he passes this power to the disciples and to the Christian community. It is still God who does the forgiving, but our friendship and warmth together with the Holy Spirit facilitate the confession and repentance. Then we can declare that forgiveness has taken place. Thus man is made whole in his heart and is at peace with God. The sin then is forgiven on earth and in heaven.

On the other hand, if a person does not confess his sin, or he does not even see that he is in sin, the fellow Christians or Church cannot forgive him and the sin remains, both on earth and in heaven (i.e., in the sinner's heart and also as a form of estrangement between himself and God).

Verses 24–28. The issue here is not the physical presence, but believing without physically seeing the reality of the spiritual presence of the risen Christ.

Verse 29. This is the climax of the Gospel and its natural ending. All that follows is editorial comment (20:30, 31; 21:23–25) or additional material (21:1–22) to supplement seeing and believing as mentioned here.

Reflection: Verse 19. How often we have experienced this mystic Presence! In the mist over a silent sea, in the rush of heavy traffic, in the sunlight streaming through the trees, in the smile of an invalid, in the rest at the end of the day! Everywhere, he is there!

It was midnight for me in the hospital two years ago. The doctor had talked of possible paralysis, a wheelchair existence, but quietly Christ was there. What the future held suddenly seemed of little import. His peace was there. I thanked him and fell asleep. Complete healing followed, but I still remember Christ's presence in that hospital room.

At a church meeting, the members had voted 243 to 241 to build a new educational wing. Terror seized the congregation. The younger crowd would now build the unit and split the church. The leaders of the majority—parents who wanted better facilities for their children—met and forewent their legal prerogative. They refused to press their advantage and announced the following Sunday that it did not seem to be God's time to build. Amazement and then tears greeted the announcement. Hardened positions softened; the peace of Christ breathed over that congregation. Both sides were suddenly united and everyone seemed to know that some-day, in God's time, the unit would be built.

When does the peace of Christ come to you? In hallowed places? In tense situations? When you have laid aside your will? When you have reached a dark impasse and there is no hope? Recall some of the times when strangely, sud-denly the Christ has made his Presence felt with you.

Verses 21–22. The disciples were assured that their Lord had risen. They believed in him. Now he could entrust them with his mission. For a long while he had been telling them that the Father had sent him. Now he can complete his work by saying, "As the Father has sent me, even so I send you." The mission would be impossible in their own strength, hence the gift of the Holy Spirit.

Do you feel a sense of mission or sentness? This risen Christ is within you. He who was sent from the Father lived a life of obedience, offered his life to the death, was raised and lives eternally with God—this Christ is your daily Com-panion. He empowers us, giving us the Holy Spirit as our Guide and Enabler.

Verse 25. John includes this story of Thomas that he may bring new faith to the Christians of his day (about A.D. 100). None of these had seen Jesus in the flesh. For the Gospel writer, they were among the blessed ones who had not seen, yet believed (v. 29). What we of the twentieth century regard as a deficit in that we cannot see the historic, physical Jesus, John sees as an asset in that we are free to encounter and embrace the risen Christ without the limitations of culture, social customs, and parochial setting.

In what way does the visible and concrete make the invis-ible more real to you? A picture? A statue? The bread and wine? In what way do these limit you?

I find myself, as I write, reaching back over the two thousand years, re-creating within me these Gospel stories. As they come alive for me and in me, Jesus is once more the sent One of God who became flesh and dwelt among us. He was obedient unto death to his Father. As I recall this, something within me bows down. I find myself saying, "My Lord and my God."

With all my heart *I believe*. I believe Jesus was sent of God, that to see him is to see God, to know him is to know God, to receive him is to receive God. As I worship, I hear his call. He who once had said, "Come and see" is now saying, "Go, as the Father has sent me, even so I send you." I am to be a partner in his mission. To assure me of his continuing Presence and power he adds, "Receive the Holy Spirit." Summarize what this Christ means to you.

XI

The Epilogue
(John 20:30–21:25)

The Purpose of John's Gospel
Read John 20:30–31

Comment: Here we learn that John selected only a small portion of what Jesus said and did for inclusion in his Gospel. The selection was guided by his aim to have people "believe that Jesus is the Christ, the Son of God, and that believing" they might "have life in his name."

We have seen Jesus portrayed as the Christ (the Messiah), the Logos, the King, as one with Father, coming from and returning to him—and also returning to his disciples as the risen Christ. The purpose of this portrayal is that we also may *believe* in order that we may have *life*.

Reflection: As I draw to the close in writing about this Gospel I am asking myself, has John's purpose been accomplished in me?

Is he truly my Christ, my King? Do I offer him just lip service or genuine reverence and obedience? When and why do I rebel? Why so often do I want my own way?

Is he the Son of God for me? Do I see his oneness with God in that he came from and went to God, in that he enfleshed on earth the Spirit of God, in that he said, "I and my Father are one"?

Finally, am I availing myself of the life he offers me? Is my faith such that I will follow him to the point of giving over my life, of my own accord, for my fellowmen in the same spirit in which he gave his? I fall far short, but I find myself saying, "My Father and my God, this is what I want more than all else in life."

The belief is in order that we "may have life in his name." There is always the tendency in religion to be onesided— a passivist or an activist, a believer or a doer. John describes Jesus as one who was both. What a believer Jesus was, believing in his Father, in himself, and in his disciples. What a doer he was, living a life of service, of faith, of fullness, of power and joy.

Christ as Host and Provider
Read John 21:1-14

Comment: This chapter is an appendix or a reinforcement of the reality of the risen Christ. It contains additional testimony to Christ's continuing presence with his disciples and emphasizes his renewal of personal relationship with them. These incidents were selected to assure the church of John's day that, in the midst of their hardships, the risen Christ was with them.

Verse 3. In times of uncertainty or trouble we tend to return to the familiar patterns of the past. The disciples had not yet sufficiently believed in the resurrection and the gift of the Holy Spirit to make these truths their basis of living. They returned to their former work as fishermen.

Verse 4. They still, in spite of the upper room experiences (20:19–29), did not recognize the risen Christ. There was a veil of mystery about his presence, a mystery symbolized by the uncertain half-light of the approaching dawn. The daylight was breaking over the landscape and the physical delineations would soon stand clear. Then they would recognize Jesus. But another light was stealing into their hearts: this Jesus with whom they had traveled through the years was indeed risen. Truly he was the Christ, the Messiah, alive forever. This truth dawned and slowly possessed them and illumined their lives.

Verse 6. The fish has become the emblem of the early church. The letters in the Greek word for "fish," *icthus,* stood for "Jesus Christ, Son of God, Savior." The catch at Galilee represented the Church blessed by the presence of Christ.

Verses 9–14. Jesus welcomed the chilled and frustrated disciples to a warm meal. A friendly dawn dispelled the long night. Likewise the risen Christ was with the early Church in their persecutions and loneliness. He brought inner sustenance and the warmth of his presence. There are overtones here of the communal meal that ultimately became the Sacrament of the Lord's Supper.

Reflection: Verse 3. How do you face loss and grief? By defensiveness? Withdrawal? Complaint? Returning to old and familiar patterns? Where are your places of withdrawal? Are these cowardly retreats from life or opportunities for regrouping preparatory to new adventure? In what way?

Verse 4. Think of some situations in which Jesus was definitely present and yet you did not recognize his presence until later. Note the approach of Jesus. There is no scolding, no act of reprisal for their desertion and Peter's denial. He sees them as hungry, chilled fishermen, disappointed after a night of fruitless work. He meets their need for warmth and food! The risen Son of God—building a fire and serving food! It is reminiscent of the washing of the disciples' feet.

Jesus was Servant *par excellence!* How have you met people who have let you down? Think of specific situations.

Verses 7–8. Note that again John was quick to see and believe (see 20:8); Peter was quick to act.

Verse 9. Note how Jesus entered into people's immediate needs. At the wedding, it was shortage of wine; for the multitude, their hunger for food; now he warmed and fed these fishermen who were cold and hungry.

Do we barge into people's lives, anxious to set them right in their thinking and reform their ways of living rather than ministering to them at the point of their needs? What does the example of Jesus say to you about his gracious and effortless reentry into the disciples' lives?

Verse 12. "Come and have breakfast." What an adroit way to mend broken fellowship, especially in the Near East where one only sat down to eat with friends. How deftly he set the stage where things might happen. Eating together tended to remove the embarrassment of the desertion. The healing could take place without self-consciousness.

Call to mind this scene on the shore of Galilee the next time you partake of the Lord's Supper. It is the Christ eating with you. He comes with the warmth of love and inner food. He is your Host and Provider. He gathers you and those partaking with you out of your loneliness into the genial fellowship of that Galilean lakeside breakfast.

Feed My Sheep

Read John 21:15–25

Comment: Verses 15–17. Jesus uses Peter's early name, Simon. He is reaching deep into Peter's being. "These" (v. 15) could refer to the fishing gear and fisherman's life, but more likely it refers to the other disciples since Jesus is grooming Peter for leadership.

Jesus used two different verbs when he asked Peter if he loved him. The first two times he used the stronger word which translates, "to love supremely." The third time he used a weaker word which might be translated, "Am I dear to you?" or "Are you my friend?" Peter used the weaker word all three times in his replies to Jesus. R. F. Weymouth in his *New Testament in Modern Speech* translates these three questions and answers as follows (italics are mine):

"Simon, son of John, do you *love me* more than these others do?" "Yes, Master. . . . you know that *you are dear to me.*"

"Simon, son of John, do you *love me?*" "Yes, Master, . . . you know that *you are dear to me.*"

"Simon, son of John, *am I dear to you?*" . . . "Master, . . . you know everything, you can see that *you are dear to me.*"

Verses 18–19. This is a prediction that Peter would die by crucifixion.

Verses 20–21. Peter was still grappling with Jesus' announcement of his eventual crucifixion.

Verse 24. It would seem that chapter 21 was added by one of John's disciples. He could well have received the material in this chapter from John himself. He is saying, in effect, "The disciple, John the Apostle, the one spoken of here, is the one who has written this Gospel. We of the present-day church, [approximately A.D. 90–100] know that what John has written is the truth."

Verse 25. There was an abundance of available material (see also 20:30). There had been a process of purposeful selection.

Reflection: Verses 15-17. Jesus began by facing Peter with a total and supreme commitment. Twice he did this and twice Peter, still hurting from his recent denial, responded with a lesser degree of loyalty. The third time, Jesus came down to and accepted Peter's degree of commitment, and used Peter's own evaluation of himself as he said, "Am I dear to you?" Jesus did not belabor Peter because he could not measure up to the standard Jesus had set. He loved Peter as he was, willingly accepted his lesser loyalty and commissioned him to feed his sheep; that is, to minister to and nurture the Church.

Does this break through with significance and power to you—that the risen Christ takes the initiative of affirming love in approaching you regardless of how much you may have failed him? That while challenging you to the highest, he accepts you as you are and calls you, with all of your faults and weaknesses, to the service and nurture of your fellow human beings? That the person you are is called into Christ's service here and now?

Christ sets an example for us to take the initiative of affirming love when approaching others. While we set before them the highest of goals, we are not to pressure people, forcing them into our molds, urging them to live up to our standards. Rather let us accept such loyalty and commitment as people are ready to give and generate in them a sense of purpose and "sentness" to minister and serve among God's people. God uses what we offer him. Will you affirm what people have and claim it for use in God's Kingdom?

Will you let Jesus ask the same questions of you that he asked of Simon Peter? Will you accept for yourself the commands that Jesus gave to Peter? Who are some of the lambs that you are tending or plan now to tend? What new, imaginative and caring steps can you introduce in your shepherding?

Verses 18–19. What do these verses say to you about your faithfulness now and also in later life? The final word is always that the Jesus of history blazed the trail for us two thousand years ago, winning the victory there and then. But this risen Christ as the Holy Spirit is with us in our pilgrimage today, offering this victory to us now and forever.

We end where we began:

In the beginning Jesus Christ was with God, and in him was life and the life was the light of men (1:1, 4). Today this Christ and God his Father have come to make their home in us, giving us this life and enabling us to walk in his light.